ess
—

Kick-Start Your Business

100 Days to a Leaner, Fitter Organisation

Robert Craven

For Cal, Jessie, Bonnie and Ben

This edition first published in Great Britain in 2005 by
Virgin Publishing Ltd
Thames Wharf Studios
Rainville Road
London
W6 9HA

First published in 2001 by Virgin Books Ltd

ISBN 0 7535 0973 3

Series Consultant: Professor David Storey
Joint Series Editors: Robert Craven, Grier Palmer

Series design by Janice Mather at Ben Cracknell Studios
Typeset by Phoenix Photosetting, Chatham, Kent
Printed and bound in Italy

Contents

Foreword by Sir Richard Branson   xi

Preface by Professor David Storey   xiii

Introduction   1

PART ONE – SORTING YOUR BUSINESS   7

Chapter One: Just how good are you really?   9
Where are you now? Where are you going?

Chapter Two: The three obsessions of successful
  organisations   27
Highly successful businesses are obsessed with
  strategy, marketing and teams. What about you?

Chapter Three: Where do you want to go?   37
Clarity about what you want to achieve makes
  planning, direction and focus much easier

Chapter Four: Strategic thinking   47
How to develop your strategy in a way that can
  help your business

Chapter Five: Strategy, shmategy – a discussion on approaching strategy   **61**
The inability of the business support community to help businesses with practical strategy leaves a big hole

Chapter Six: Marketing   **71**
Simple marketing is one of the keys to success. What you need to be thinking about to get your marketing in order

Chapter Seven: Bright marketing   **89**
How to start to make your 'bright marketing' company. Be brighter and smarter than the competition. The focus is on getting your brand and offering truly sorted

Chapter Eight: Focus your people on customers   **103**
A major part of success in business is getting your people to buy into the importance of customers

Chapter Nine: Leaders as band leaders and surfers   **111**
Business leaders need the skills of jazz band leaders to direct a business. Pick the right current and be agile in your reactions and decisions

Chapter Ten: Running the business   **121**
The successful work *on* rather than *in* their business. The board and the directors' roles are little understood, resulting in the 'headless chicken' syndrome

Chapter Eleven: Sort finance   **131**
At the heart of every business, the money and
the numbers must be understood. A brief
examination of some key concepts for running
rather than auditing a successful business

Chapter Twelve: Growth and balance   **143**
Growth means more staff, but at which level?
And what about staff development and
motivation?

Chapter Thirteen: Habits of effectiveness   **151**
How can you be more effective? Here are some
of the common traits of the 'effective'

Chapter Fourteen: The psychology of success   **163**
There are some key similarities in the psychology
of successful managers. What is it that they
do that makes them different from the rest?

**Chapter Fifteen: Innovation – getting out of
your box**   **169**
Innovation and entrepreneurship go hand-in-hand.
Revitalise entrepreneurship and get innovation
into your business

**Chapter Sixteen: MORFA – looking at business
projects and business plans**   **183**
A simple framework for evaluating either a start-up
or a business project

**Chapter Seventeen: Helping your business to
measure up – the scorecard**   **191**
A powerful device for measuring and implementing
your strategy

Chapter Eighteen: Crunch questions   201
Some really searching questions and one-liners to
   get you ready for the 100-day workout

PART TWO: THE 100-DAY WORKOUT   213

Session One: FiMO/RECoIL & SNOW
   workshop – just how good are you?   217

Session Two: Vision setting   220

Session Three: Key questions in strategy   224

Session Four: Business purpose audit   225

Session Five: Market environment audit   226

Session Six: Competition audit   227

Session Seven: Individual competitor audits   228

Session Eight: Industry attractiveness   231

Session Nine: Culture audit   232

Session Ten: Long-term plans   234

Session Eleven: Organisation structure audit   235

Session Twelve: Short-term plans   236

Session Thirteen: Finance workout   239

Session Fourteen: Bright-marketing workout   241

Session Fifteen: Balanced business scorecard   246

Session Sixteen: One-page business plan and
   action planning   248

Session Seventeen: The best year yet   249

Postscript   251

Bibliography   253

Featured growing companies   255

Useful websites and addresses   257

Glossary of terms   263

Index   267

Foreword
by Sir Richard Branson

I have always learnt my business on the job – from setting up *Student* magazine way back in 1967 right through to running the Virgin Group in the twenty-first century as one of the biggest brands in the world – rather than from a book, which makes it novel to be writing this foreword for the new editions of the Virgin Business Guide series.

I wouldn't call myself a marketing expert or a finance professional, however, nor am I the best person to do each and every job in the company – that's what I employ great staff for! And on a day-to-day basis, whatever the size of your company, you'll probably have advisers for all aspects of your business – from planning your next move to marketing and PR; from finance to problem solving and how to look after your customers – and these advisers are essential. At Virgin I do believe it is *my* job, though, to make the best possible decisions and that is only feasible if I know enough about each aspect of my business to make informed choices.

Learning from other people's business successes and failures can be an essential part of your own success. When I've experienced setbacks in my own business life, I have picked myself up again and had another go using the knowledge that I've gained from that failure. I have also always found advice from someone who's tried something similar before you – such as from Freddie Laker of Laker Airways when it came to running Virgin Atlantic and dealing with some of the early problems we encountered, or from Per

Lindstrand, who introduced me to ballooning and taught me much of what I know about it – one of the most important aspects of running my business. Even if, when it comes to it, I make my own decisions.

This series of books, in conjunction with Warwick Business School, is all written by businessmen and women who have been in business themselves and are therefore aware of the importance of information and the pitfalls you might come across. Not only that, but they include advice, ideas and case studies from many other successful and less successful businesspeople to help you.

Robert Craven's *Kick-Start Your Business* covers an essential part of running a business – transforming your plans for the business into actions, which will 'turn your business into a powerhouse' by recovering some of the passion and nimbleness of the small business to make your growing business 'more effective and more profitable'. Often businesses, especially those that have grown larger, can become stale, with processes and results remaining static over time leading to inertia in the decision-making processes. I've found that, in these situations, the business in question often needs a boost – a kick-start to greater success in the future.

The figures speak for themselves – about half of small businesses fail in the first four years – so in whatever industry you work you need all the help you can get to succeed. And, above all, you should be having fun. Use these books as your tools, follow the advice and then make your own decisions – after all, you're the boss!

Preface

Robert Craven is one of Warwick Business School's most highly regarded presenters. His animated, action-packed style demands participation. Robert does not give his audience the option of sitting back and merely reflecting.

I wondered how this presentation style would translate into words on pages and was delighted to find that the reader of this volume is as bullied and cajoled into participation as is the listener. The business owner, at whom this book is directed, is forced to estimate scores out of ten in the key areas of their own business. It is these scores that Robert Craven uses to focus discussion on what he regards as the key areas of finance, marketing and operations.

Equally, in examining the potential of the business for future development the reader is forced to score their business in areas such as resources, experience, controls and assistance, ideas and innovation and leadership. The reader is constantly challenged to provide reasons why one score is higher or lower than another, or even to ask others in the business to undertake the same exercise to see if scores tally. The scores help both to stimulate dialogue and to focus Robert Craven's attention on the key issues.

If the first key characteristic of the book is its emphasis upon participation, the second is on simplicity. Robert Craven emphasises that running a business is not rocket science, but neither should the thought needed to run a successful business be underestimated. The scores which he makes the reader estimate for themselves are only the basis for identifying the strengths and weaknesses of the business. What he correctly stresses is that owners have to make clear-minded decisions in the context of good information. Such clear-mindedness comes only by stripping away the inevitable day-to-day concerns and answering the questions raised by Robert Craven.

The third characteristic Robert Craven emphasises is that responsibility for the business, both its success and also its lack of success, is down to those who run it. If the plaudits are laid at the door of the business owner when it is successful then so are the failings when it does not succeed.

Finally, I hope the readers also like the consistent structure of the chapters in this book. I found concluding with 'Frequently asked questions' particularly valuable.

So, if you want a book which makes you think about your own business and which provides genuine real-life examples derived almost entirely from small businesses with which Robert Craven has personally come in contact, then this book is for you.

What the book will not do is to tell you what to do. Instead it will force you to ask yourself questions about your own business, enabling you then to either find out what you don't know or make the best possible decisions on the limited information available. That must be of value.

Professor David Storey
Director, Centre for Small and Medium Sized Enterprises
Warwick Business School, University of Warwick

Introduction

This book has been written as a result of over twenty years of running businesses and helping other people to make their businesses become successful. There seem to be common ingredients that the successful companies consistently exhibit. There are certain things that these companies focus on.

What has become apparent over time is that these 'recipes for success' are usually fairly simple and uncomplicated. The industry of business advisers, consultants, academics and professionals seems to have shrouded the essential skills behind a veil of smoke and mystery. This book takes these recipes, these magic formulae, and tells you how to apply the alchemy.

Whether your business is large or small, here are the tools you need to sort your business, to turn your business into a powerhouse: tools, resources and contacts to transform plans into specific actions.

Running a business can be a lonely affair. Too much to do, too little time. There's always the danger that you start to feel like a 'busy fool'; it is so easy to think that you might have lost the plot.

Kick-Start Your Business is a practical, hands-on approach to putting your affairs in order and getting your business to work for you, and includes a series of proven worksheets to 'sort your business'. *Kick-Start Your Business* takes you a quantum leap beyond do-it-yourself business guides and shows you how to apply your ideas with excellence and originality.

This is much more than a book: it is a programme, and for some it becomes a way of life. The book is made up of commentary and worksheets, a website and a live discussion forum. It contains a route map to sort out your business for the future.

Your company and your future may depend on this book!

Who is this book for?

This book is aimed at anyone who is running their own business or someone else's business.

Running your own business is no mean achievement. Sometimes it feels as if you are running up the 'down' escalator. Whether you work alone or employ ten or fifteen staff, the principles in this book will help you to become more effective and more profitable.

It is also aimed at the growing business that is trying to become more businesslike.

Business growth creates its own problems. The pressures of increasing your sales and maintaining profitability and cash flow create their own potential nightmare scenario. This book has been written as a result of working with just such companies.

This book is also aimed at the larger business that is trying to become more entrepreneurial.

Politicians celebrate 'entrepreneurship' without actually defining what it is. As businesses grow and mature, they do tend to introduce systems and procedures that stunt the innovation and flair. They lose the passion that is common in younger businesses. Regain some of that nimbleness and the sense of excitement that goes with it.

Finally, it is aimed at the business that feels that is has come up against a glass ceiling.

Despite our best endeavours, sometimes the task seems to defeat us. This 'running out of puff' is common. Maybe it is time for a rethink – re-evaluation of what is really going on and the possible alternatives that are available. We will look at how you can break through those glass ceilings.

What this book is not

This book is not a business-school textbook. It has not been written with any kind of student in mind! It has not been written with the intention of helping you pass any exams. It is not full of abstract theories. It is not full of remote case studies that seem to bear little relation to the reality of running a business.

 ## Why this book was written

I have spent twenty years working with businesses of all sizes. I have been asked to act in various roles: as coach, trainer, expert adviser, catalyst, stern critic, consultant, and nonexecutive director. In a nutshell, I am asked to make the companies more entrepreneurial and/or make them more businesslike. I am fed up with theoretical rhetoric, and so my style has always been to offer practical solutions that lead to tangible results.

I am constantly asked to recommend books that will assist people to grow and develop their businesses. I have found a few that have come close to what was required but never one that would do the trick.

This book is the book that I have always been looking for to help people run better businesses. I hope that it will help you to run yours.

Is this book any different from the rest?

For a start, this book is focused on methods and tools that are known to work in businesses like your own. This book was created with the co-operation (and feedback) of thousands of businesses that have applied these tools to their own businesses. The tools work.

The book is peppered with case studies and live examples of the issues that you are dealing with. You can follow how some of these businesses have developed on our website at www.kick-starters.com

The book is divided into two distinct but complementary sections:

> ■ **Part One** is a commentary about how to look at and improve your business: ideas, thoughts, case studies (genuine examples).
>
> ■ **Part Two** is about what you need to do to look at and improve your business: worksheets, workouts and tools to make you think about your business and its future.

When you buy this book you get access to a web-based discussion forum where you can share your business issues with other like-minded businesspeople. Sign up now and join the Kick-starters business community – express your views or ask for advice and support: www.egroups.com/group/kick-starters.

How to use this book

This book is designed to be used as a tool to improve your business. You can use the book to suit your style or read it from cover to cover. Or you can skim Part One and then focus all your efforts on Part Two, the 100-day plan. Alternatively, you can go straight to the 100-day plan in Part Two and start work on it now and ignore Part One. Or you can dip into any part of the book and start applying the 'lessons' to your business right now.

Different ways of doing the 100-day workout

The serious stuff starts here. A hundred days is just over fourteen weeks. This book does not set out to tell you how to sort your business in a step-by-step way – 'today you do this, tomorrow you do that'. The book will not spoon-feed you: you still need to put in the hours, the hard work. You can decide for yourself what is the best way for you to use the book.

Kick-Start gives you all the tools of analysis that you need to transform your business. The hard bit is actually taking your dreams and putting them into action. So, while you are given models and case studies to show you how to kick-start your business, the real part, the serious work will still have to be done by you.

You will need to set aside time to reflect on what you have been doing and what you want to do for the future. More importantly, all the analysis in the world is an entire waste of time without decisions and action. This book endeavours to help you make those decisions and offers you examples, encouragement and support in putting your plans into action. The book, however, will not make it happen. It is you who will do that.

The 100-day workout has seventeen sessions, or exercises, which are estimated to take roughly eighteen to twenty hours if you do them all as instructed. Each session gives an indicative timing and you can adjust this to suit you own needs.

Depending on your specific needs, you can:

> ■ Read Part One first, taking, say, two weeks, and then do the sessions in Part Two, say, two a week (for those who are a little more reflective and want to be more thorough).
>
> ■ Go straight to Part Two, the sessions, and plough through them as quickly as possible, and use Part One to check you are approaching the exercises in the right way. This could be done at the speed of, say, three to four sessions per week.
>
> ■ Pick the areas that you think you need to improve and read the relevant section in Part One and do the relevant sessions in Part Two.
>
> ■ Take two full days out of the office and work your way through the sessions as instructed. Spend the remaining 98 days implementing your new plans.

100-day plans are very powerful. To stick to the 100-day planning concept your time could look as follows:

Week 1:   Scan Part One of the book.
Week 2:   Focus your attention on your key areas for concern in Part One.
Week 3:   Focus and decide – use Part Two sessions to arrive at a plan for the remainder of the period.
Week 4:   Decide and communicate your new plan.

Weeks 5–7:   Act on the plans.

Week 8:   Review progress to date. Celebrate your successes. Learn from your experiences. Adjust plans accordingly.

Weeks 9–10:   Use revised plans to act.

Week 11:   Review progress to date. Celebrate your successes. Learn from your experiences. Adjust or create new plans accordingly.

Weeks 12–13: Use revised plans to act.

Week 14:   Review progress to date. Celebrate your successes. Learn from your experiences. Adjust or create new plans accordingly.

Use the book however *you* want. My only plea is that you do use it as a lever to improve your business. Use the web-based discussion forum to let me and your fellow readers know what happens to you – share your success and your failures and what you have learned.

Your business will not change unless you act – action is at the heart of this book. *I* can only show you the tools to use; *you* must use them.

The mere fact that you feel driven to buy the book suggests that you want to make some changes. Buying the book is not enough. To get any kind of benefit you need to work with your team to make the difference that makes the difference. This work will pay off dividends.

Go For It!

– Robert Craven
rc@robert-craven.com
Bath, November 2004

PART ONE

SORTING YOUR BUSINESS

CHAPTER ONE

Just how good are you really?

Before you can talk about what you wish to become, you need to have a clear idea of where you are now . . . and what your potential to grow, your capability, is like. Using the FiMO/RECoIL Framework, you can identify strengths and weaknesses in the business and assess your capability to grow. This framework has now been applied to thousands of businesses with staggering results. It really tells you where you need to concentrate your efforts. And, if you lie to it, you are simply cheating yourself.

When you look at your own business, you need to somehow evaluate what is really going on. A framework is required to assist you to evaluate your performance to date and your capability to develop the business. There are plenty of business frameworks and models available from consultants and business schools. The trouble with them is that they do not always help you to create a better business.

This chapter introduces a framework that looks primarily at the business itself. This framework is referred to by the acronyms FiMO and RECoIL.

FiMO/RECoIL is a framework for looking at *your* business. It can be used:

- To evaluate the strengths and weaknesses of your business
- By counsellors working with businesses
- To write up business healthchecks
- By bankers to evaluate businesses
- To open up discussion within/with a company to discuss/agree the 'state of play'

Most businesses seem to have some kind of plan, or idea about what they are trying to do. Before you can look at future plans, you need to know where the business is now and what its capability (its potential) to develop is like.

To address these issues the framework is divided into two sections:

1 The company's *performance to date*
2 The company's *capability to grow*

Measuring your company's performance to date

When businesspeople are asked 'What measures should be used to assess your company's performance to date?', the same list of answers is usually put forward, give or take one or two differences.

The list offered includes measures such as:

- Turnover in units and pounds
- Gross and net profit margins
- Return on capital employed
- Liquidity
- Cash flow
- Stock
- Wages bill, and so forth

While these financial measures are commendable as a list, to some degree they miss some of the point. What really matters is far more than just the financials.

Paul, the accountant, would come out with a statement like, 'Finance is the engine of the business without which there would be no reason for the company's being in existence; cash flow is the oil that makes the business work, and therefore finance is the only thing that really matters.'

But still I feel drawn to say, 'Poppycock! There's more to understanding the business's performance than simply the financials. While I don't dispute the importance of finance, you need to recognise that it is simply a consequence of two other factors, marketing and operations . . .'

So, why do we always go to the financials when asked to evaluate performance to date? There are several reasons.

The first is that financials are easy to read and to measure – they somehow give a scientific and objective feel as the numbers are compared and contrasted.

The second reason lies with how businesses have received their teachings to date. Businesses get their knowledge from a limited number of sources. Unfortunately, the knowledge that is shared with them is often based on theory and academic models rather than experience and easily applicable tools to assist you.

A third reason is that most of the financial information is not necessarily accurate, up to date or measuring the right things.

For advice about running businesses, the traditional sources of help have been the accountants, banks and universities, who usually have whole departments specialising in the use and application of financial measures to businesses. It is almost as if a conspiracy of these three parties has misled businesspeople to think and believe that the financials are the only thing that really count.

One of the biggest mistakes made by business schools is the artificial separation of business into numerous functions or categories of expertise such as finance, marketing, production and operations management, strategy, human resources, industrial relations and organisational behaviour. While these functional titles may be appropriate for expert or academic study, or even reflect the functions within a multinational business, the reality is that in the majority of businesses none of these things happens within a vacuum, independent of the others.

Most business textbooks and studies look at a specific part of the business – for instance, marketing or finance. This approach makes study (and analysis) easier. Unfortunately, the resultant output does not accurately reflect the reality of trying to run a real business.

A more accurate understanding of the business's performance to date is to recognise that finance reflects the marketing and operations performance. Finance is a consequence of marketing and operations performance.

Introducing the *FiMO* framework for looking at 'performance to date'

The framework we use to assess a company's performance to date is known as FiMO: Finance (Fi), Marketing (M), Operations and production (O). The FiMO framework gives a 'holistic' view of the business.

A specialist in marketing will look for and see marketing issues as the key to a business situation; and an accountant will look for and see the financial issues. The FiMO framework gives us a much more balanced view of how the business has performed.

So you need to recognise that we have three interlocking and overlapping functions, both coexisting and interdependent. The image to be held in mind is that of a juggler – when all the balls move smoothly then there are no problems, but, if one ball starts to misbehave, then chaos ensues.

Alternatively, imagine that the three functions are bonded and intertwined like the neutrons and protons in an atom. They are all interrelated and the equilibrium depends on the various constituent parts each performing its role (in relation to the others). If one part (or neutron) becomes unstable then the rest will also be affected.

What we mean by marketing and operations in this context

Marketing is all about getting customers and selling to them. And there are as many measures of marketing as there are measures of finance.

Operations is all about producing the service or product. It is all about 'doing'. And there are as many measures of operations as there are of finance.

Experience of running businesses suggests that, more often than not, you are preoccupied with the making and the selling. In other words, marketing and operations. Without the ability to find customers and sell to them (the marketing), and the actual production or delivery of the service or product (the operations), then there would be very little to measure!

ACTION POINT

Right, now, score your business! Take each heading, and give your business a score out of ten (where 0 is a very low score and 10 is a very high score).

How do the scores work?

> Scores of 2 or 3 suggest that there is something seriously wrong.
>
> Scores of 4 or 5 or 6 suggest mediocrity.
>
> Scores of 8 or 9 suggest that you are pretty good if not 'world-class'. You may need to find some evidence to support your case. I would always question and challenge such scores.

In fact, write down the scores in the book, right here, on the page. After all this is a working book, not a precious book to be kept clean. Mark any pages in the book that you find of value.

So, here goes ... mark your scores out of ten. Remember that this scoring system is subjective: it should be your gut response. By definition, this process is a little ambiguous, and that is because we are interested in the process, the discussion, about what the scores mean and how they can be improved.

Heading:	Your score:
Finance	
Marketing	
Operations	

As soon as you enter a number you (or your colleagues) can argue why the score given was either too high or too low. For instance, if you give yourselves 7 for finance, why haven't you given yourself 8 or 6? What would you need to do to improve the score? What makes you so sure that you get only a 7? Is it 7 and improving, or is it 7 and getting worse?

This is a real process. How can you justify your scores? Where is the evidence? What would you need to do to improve it? Why has it not been better in the past? Such a way of scoring immediately suggests where there may be room for improvement.

If you have filled in the FiMO scores for your business then you can see how it gets you to think through and justify the scores you have given. Try talking this through with a colleague. How would they score the business under the FiMO headings?

The figure below fleshes out some of the components under each heading.

The Performance To Date (FiMO)

Finance	Marketing	Operations
turnover (sales/units)	advertising spend	output per worker
break-even point	selling effectiveness	output per machine
gross profit margin	customer retention	age of equipment
net profit margin	new accounts won	set-up times
liquidity ratios	repeat business	down time
ROCE	new products	absenteeism
debtor/creditor days	brand perception	staff turnover
gearing/interest cover	(by competition)	staff training
	brand perception	defect rate
	(by customers)	performance advantage
	market position	

This list is by no means exhaustive but it gives you an indication of the sorts of things that you can measure to address the company's performance to date. All the qualities are relatively easy to measure and, taken together, these measures give a good indication of the 'state of play'.

Case study

The Motorised Trike Company started to manufacture and sell tricycles with small motors that could carry up to three adults. After three years in business, things were going badly. They could, if needed, make hundreds per week; the costings suggested that there would be large profits to be made if sales would increase to above the break-even point. Clive, the owner, filled in his FiMO score sheet with the following explanations:

FINANCE: 5. 'The financial model can work. Profit per unit after the first 100 per week will run at $50 per unit. Based on sales of 500 a week at $125 each, we are looking at a gross profit of about $50,000!!!'

MARKETING: 2. 'Our promotional material is spot on but at the end of the day we are starting to think that no one actually wants this product.'

OPERATIONS: 5 'Our processes and systems are perfect: we could make 500 or even 1,000 units per week and employ no additional staff. But, to date, performance has been on the quiet side.'

On reflection, Clive realised that basically his marketing had failed – no one actually wanted his product. (Marketing is about seeing the business through the customers' eyes!) Despite his brilliant financial model and his slick factory, the reality was that he had not made a product the market wanted. Talking through the FiMO enabled him to see the reality, the truth, the fundamental weakness in his business. He could now come to terms with the fact that business closure could become inevitable, unless he could use the same financial and operations systems but a different product that the market actually wanted

Case study

Specialist Oils sold £3 million each year of a unique imported engine oil/cleanser to the car manufacturing industry. The oil was imported by ship from South Africa. Profits were very high and there was a captive audience because of the oil's unique cleaning power. Oil was delivered in large drums and passed on to customers in the same form! Jerry, the owner employed three drivers who delivered the oil barrels around the UK.

FINANCE: 9. Profits were really high.

MARKETING: 6. There was little visible marketing activity, but rather a series of close relationships.

OPERATIONS: 7. Simple and effective.

When pursued about why operations had scored only 7, Jerry admitted that he would not give a higher score because: 'We have only the one product but it is always delivered to us on time. In fact I have never actually met the supplier – he gets me to deposit money in a Swiss bank account and that's how we do business: I call him, he quotes a price, I pay, he delivers. That was how it began and that is how we continue to do business.'

On reflection, Jerry re-scored his business (9, 5, 5) and realised that, in truth, the whole business was trading on shaky ground. He was too dependent on one supplier and one product. He had made exceptional profits but it was time to protect the potential downside of the business and start to dilute his dependence on the South African connection. Three years later, turnover was £3.5 million: Jerry had introduced a whole series of equally profitable ancillary products to his range; his competition for the oil had begun to steal some of his customers. His move away from dependence on the single product probably saved him.

These case studies show how the use of the framework makes you ask questions of the business and this guides you to start making some sense of what is otherwise a series of disconnected ideas and thoughts.

The potential to grow – RECoIL

When looking at a business, to assess whether it has 'what it takes', the measures become incredibly subjective and woolly.

You will often hear phrases such as 'You just look 'em in the eye and you can see whether they've got it or not' or 'Some people smell of success, you just know that they've got what it takes.' Well, there must be some way to be more substantial in establishing a company's potential and capability. The RECoIL part of the FiMO/RECoIL framework gives you a series of headings that will help you to assess the business's potential or capability to grow.

FiMO uses relatively objective measures to evaluate a company's performance to date; RECoIL, examining the company's potential to grow, looks for far more subjective measures. This part of the framework is based on the ideas of Allan Gibb from Durham University Business School. The measures are not highly sophisticated and are not put into sophisticated business-school-speak; but this part of the framework is incredibly powerful.

RECoIL stands for Resources (R), Experience (E), Controls and systems (Co), Ideas and innovation (I), Leadership (L). RECoIL examines these headings and considers the headings in terms of how appropriate the qualities are for whatever the business is trying to do.

Resources

Essentially, resources can be divided up like this:

- Financial resources, which include: own resources, assets, liabilities (cash, profit retention, share ownership); other sources of finance (HP, borrowing, family), creditworthiness for borrowing.
- Physical resources, such as land, factories, offices, plant, machinery (including age and appropriateness). How appropriate is it for the scale of works and type of operations?
- Human resources, notably your people, your staff and management team. What training needs might you have? What gaps might you have in your 'skills inventory'?
- Intellectual resources such as patents, inventions and databases.
- Technology flexibility and capability.

Experience

Experience of running/growing a business of its current size, employing this number of people, in this market, borrowing, selling to these customers, introducing new products/services to the market, this stage of the economic cycle. Experience of going into new markets, using external agents and advisers, and of managing growth. Experience appropriate to what is required by the future needs of the business.

Controls and systems

'Controls and systems' refers to financial measurement, monitoring and control, hardware and software systems, as well as invoicing and payment and quality systems. Does the organisation collect the right information in order to make properly informed decisions? Does the organisation know what the right information is? How appropriate is the organisational structure? The issue, again, is about appropriateness of the controls and systems to the requirements of an organisation at its particular stage of growth.

Ideas and innovation

By 'ideas', we are really referring to profitable ideas that can be taken to market. It is very common for the entrepreneurial mind to have a surplus of novel ideas, but the issues are:

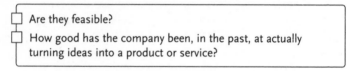

☐ Are they feasible?
☐ How good has the company been, in the past, at actually turning ideas into a product or service?

By 'innovation', we mean the business's ability to use innovation to its advantage, to put innovative ideas into practice; this could be innovative marketing, products, systems, processes, or any way in which the business tries to get ahead.

Leadership

'Leadership' refers not just to the capabilities of the leader or leaders of the organisation, but also to the direction that the company might have with respect to its focus, vision, and mission. As a result, leadership can be embodied in a team or a series of individuals or the plans, and not necessarily just the managing director alone! It is also central to understand how well the messages about the organisation's focus, vision and mission have been communicated throughout the company.

Using RECoIL

By taking the five RECoIL boxes into account, you can start to build up an understanding of the company's potential strengths and weaknesses. Decisions are made as a result of good information – the more you understand what makes your organisation tick, the better informed, and more reliable will be your decision-making.

When you score the business, you might get marks out of 10 like this:

Resources:	6 (financial: 6; physical: 7; human: 5; intellectual: 4; technology: 4)
Experience:	5
Controls:	5
Ideas:	6
Leadership:	8

Case study

This shows how to apply the FiMO/RECoIL Framework. Tim had set up XTC Ltd six years ago. XTC currently turned over £4.5 million employing 45 workers making filters for industrial chimney stacks. Tim currently held 46 per cent of the UK manufacturing of industrial chimney-stack filters in the UK.

The business was not profitable and had never made a profit. Tim's dad had put about £50,000 into the business each year, for the last three or four years. So, despite good turnover, profitability was suspect. With respect to marketing, the 46 per cent market share suggests that they must be doing something right, although they might have bought market share at the cost of profit. Tim never specified which market he had 46 per cent of, and he never made reference to competitive products, substitutes or compliments to his product.

Tim did not really trust his team. His marketing director was allowed to do little marketing, as Tim insisted on doing all the selling himself. Tim's workshop manager was Ken. Ken was described as a 'control freak', incapable of taking criticism. He was unable to accept that the product was pretty standard and that it

Growth Potential/Capability (RECoIL)

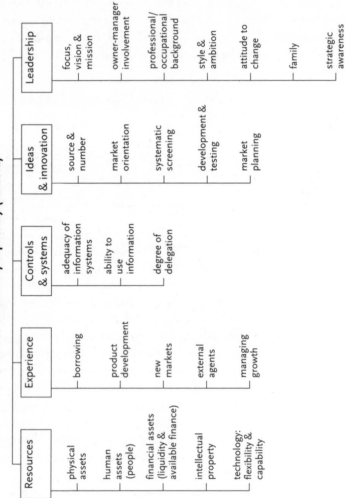

The FiMO/RECoIL Framework

THE PERFORMANCE
The company's performance to date?

| Finance | Marketing | Operations |

THE CAPABILITY
The company's potential/bases for growth

| Resources | Experience | Controls & systems | Ideas & innovation | Leadership |

did not need to be made by hand or on a bespoke basis. It would be far easier to manufacture standard sizes and then tailor the specification by the use of simple brackets and shoulders – the customers wouldn't mind and the entire process would be much more straightforward. To be blunt, his team's work quality was reflected in the sheer number of complaints and reworks required!

Tim confessed, 'Ken is screwing up my business.' Ken was threatening to leave and join the competition, which Tim could have encouraged him to do; but, no, he was panicking and trying to hold on to him!

In terms of financial resources, XTC had Tim's dad (and his bank account!). They had precious little as physical resources, as their current plant was essentially a large shed with a few relatively unsophisticated tools inside it. Human resources was the team of forty staff who were not very highly skilled, just like the management team.

When looking at experience we need to consider the appropriateness for the future. Tim and his team had learned little from their experience of running the business – Tim had no experience of leading a management team and preferred to shirk his formal responsibilities where possible. He was often heard saying that he could earn more in America with considerably less stress. My thought was, Why don't you? Remember, he had not deliberately grown the business and did not really understand what was going on!

Controls and systems were an absolute disaster. The company didn't like to send invoices because, more often than not, some additional work might be required. Also, Tim found money to be a bit of a taboo subject. As a result, invoices were posted late, so payments arrived late, which meant that Tim's cheques were slow in being sent out – by this stage, suppliers would take only cash-on-delivery jobs from Tim because some of his cheques had bounced. Because suppliers were being tight, XTC found it harder and harder to make and deliver products to their customers on time. And on and on went the vicious cycle.

Tim had tons of ideas for products and services from special yo-yos to leachate systems for landfill sites. How many of these were workable was an entirely different matter. As a leader, Tim was pretty hopeless and never took an objective view. He felt that everyone was getting at him and that no one really respected him.

Tim appeared to have little or no capabilities appropriate for the future. But does this make the business into a 'basket case'? Should Tim be told to close up shop and go home, or is there some way of turning around the enterprise?

If you were to mark XTC, you might give them marks like this:

Performance to date:

Finance	4
Marketing	5
Operations	4

Capability to grow:

Resources	5+	(financial: 5; physical: 6; human: 5; intellectual: 4; technology: 4)
Experience	3	
Controls and systems	3	
Ideas and innovation	6	
Leadership	1	

The framework shows us where XTC is weak and suggests a possible solution. If Tim were to employ an effective general manager, he would be freed up to do what he loves, which is the product invention and creation. A good general manager, by definition, would instigate clear focus, vision and mission, good tight controls and systems. They would bring with them the experience required to drive such a business. With the bearable resources that exist, the operations function would get sorted out and a focus for the marketing activities would be established. As a result of this, the financials would be turned around.

And that was exactly what happened.

Tim was made chief executive and put in charge of R&D. A general manager was employed to run the business. He was someone who had experience of running a business of this size who was thorough and professional in his approach.

The production manager, Ken, was made redundant. Twenty-five other jobs were also lost and this made no impact on output levels. Makes you wonder what they had been doing before!

Conclusion

The framework is an incredibly easy and simple-to-use tool. It also has a depth to it, which is missed at first sight. Simple frameworks are worth their weight in gold – they have a certain intuitive logic and attractiveness and are easy and very effective to apply.

ACTION POINT

Right, now, score your business! Take each heading, and give your business a score out of ten.

Heading:	Your score:
Resources	
Experience	
Controls and systems	
Ideas and innovation	
Leadership	

How to use the complete FiMO/RECoIL framework

1 Work alone (or score yourself) and then show the scores to a colleague/adviser.

2 Get your colleague/adviser to challenge you about each score.

- Where's the proof?
- What would you need to do to get another point?
- Are you sure that it isn't a point lower?
- How are you going to get the extra point?
- What is the trend behind the score?

3 Any scores less that 5 need to be discussed properly – these are real problem areas. What can be done?

4 Make recommendations based on current scores and future ambitions. Be aware of the consequences of each change.

Case study

The highly successful architectural and interior-office-design company Marshall Cummings Marsh, employs fifty people. The FiMO/RECoIL framework was used as the focus of an awayday for the senior team. The framework allowed the team to discuss and share their feelings and thoughts about the past and the future. Hazel Marsh, the MD, saw her team come together to work on the future options with a common, agreed understanding of the current situation.

Case study

Arcadia, the importer and retailer of fashion items, with several shops in London, used the FiMO/RECoIL framework to agree strengths and weaknesses within the business. As a family business with a track record of growth, the business needed to take stock of the situation before purchasing another shop in a prime retail high street. Jane Caesarea and her team used the framework to get to grips with key areas for improvement in the business; they were able to identify their true strengths and recognise the weaknesses that needed to be dealt with. It gave added confidence to the team's decision-making process.

Case study

A London cathedral's management team used the framework to come to terms with the need to run a professional organisation. The framework was used to identify and recognise where the organisation needed to make improvement.

Case study

The senior management team of Fastbake, part of a global bakery conglomerate, are responsible for supplying bakery goods such as garlic bread to supermarket chains. They used the framework in preparation for a presentation of the 'New Business Plan' to the new group managing director. Using the framework, the team were able to decide which strengths needed to be capitalised upon.

Checklist – just how good are you really?

- ☐ Have you got an agreed understanding of just how good your business really is?
- ☐ How do your scores compare with those of your competitors?
- ☐ How would your customers score your business?
- ☐ What is the trend – are you improving, staying the same or getting worse?
- ☐ Have you got evidence to support the way that you would score your business?

Frequently asked questions

Q. What if I don't know how to score a box?

A. Well, that tells you that here is a field where you simply don't know enough and need to do some research.

Q. Do 'finance' and 'marketing' and 'operations' simply refer to those functions/departments and how they perform?

A. No. You are scoring the process, the performance, and not the department. For instance, in finance you are looking at the business's financial performance, not the performance of the

finance function. In marketing, you are looking at how good
your marketing is, and how well you perform in the market.

Q. Are there some common trends that often recur?

A. Yes.

> ■ Poor leadership normally leads on to poor controls. After
> all, if you don't know where you are going, then it is
> unlikely that you will know what to measure!
> ■ A low score in leadership and/or controls normally leads
> on to a poor score in marketing and/or operations.
> ■ Younger companies tend to be operations-driven or
> marketing-driven.

Some tips for interpreting the scores?

This scoring system is all about process – most of the value comes
out of discussing the scores and their implications . . .

> ☐ Always be critical of lots of high scores.
> ☐ Always check that the scorer isn't being too self-critical.
> ☐ Always check for the trend of each score. Is it 6 and rising or 6
> and falling?
> ☐ Always look for evidence to support each score.
> ☐ Any score that sits outside the average of the rest must be
> examined carefully. For instance, a score of finance 8,
> marketing 8, operations 2 is very suspicious to me. Unless you
> are in a monopoly situation, the finance score should really be
> an average of the marketing and operations scores. Finance is a
> consequence of marketing and operations performance.

Summary

Before you can talk about what you wish to become, you need to
have a clear idea of where you are now and what your potential to
grow, your capability, is like.

Using the FiMO/RECoIL framework, you identify strengths (and
neutrals) and weaknesses in the business as well as assess the capability to grow. It tells you where you need to concentrate your efforts.

CHAPTER TWO

The three obsessions of successful organisations

Business failure is attributable to one key factor in 99.9 per cent of cases: the owner-manager or the management team. In other words, YOU! You hold the key to your business success and you hold the key to your business failure. The highly successful have an obsessive focus on three key things – do you? And finally, why do most businesses ignore the obvious?

Why do businesses fail?

Next time you are in a pub and you overhear that inevitable conversation about business failure, listen carefully. Listen to the language. Also listen to the reasons given for the business failure. You can assemble the standard list from almost any pub in the country, and it looks something like this:

The real-ale pub list of reasons (or excuses) for business failure

Pick any five or six of the reasons given below:

- 'The bank pulled the plug'
- 'A key customer refused to pay'
- 'The interest rate on loans'
- 'Increases in rent'
- 'Couldn't get/keep the staff'
- 'The competition were better/faster/cheaper/nicer . . .'
- 'Couldn't afford to invest . . .'
- 'New products of competitors were better/faster/cheaper/nicer'
- 'Couldn't keep the customers'
- 'The product wouldn't sell'

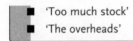

- 'Too much stock'
- 'The overheads'

The real reason for business failure, in 99.9 per cent of cases, is managerial incompetence. The responsibility lies in the hands of the person/people running the business. After all it is the job of management to look after all of the above. It is no one else's job!

Most business failures tend to blame everyone else but themselves for their misfortune. (Psychologists call this an 'external locus' of control.) On the other hand, most business successes tend to take full responsibility for the success and the failures of their business. This is called an 'internal locus' of control. When push comes to shove, the successful recognise that it is up to them (and no one else) to make a success of their business. They don't use victim language to describe their position and they don't blame others. They look, they decide, they act.

The three things that highly successful businesses are obsessed with

The three things that the highly successful are obsessed with are:

- Strategy
- Marketing
- Teams

A vast quantity of research concludes that it is these three little words that hold the key to the success of the business. The meaning and power that come from understanding these concepts will determine your future.

By focusing on the three key concepts, it does not mean that other concepts (product, finance, cash and so on) are not important. No, what is being said, by isolating these three fields, is that the highly successful business is preoccupied with them as well as being pretty good at the 'other stuff'. It is this preoccupation that is present in each year's winners of the various 'Entrepreneur of the Year' awards. And it is when a business loses these obsessions that it starts to go 'off the boil' – the magic seems to stop working when the business ceases to be driven by this triad.

Before proceeding with the rest of the book, it will make sense to give relatively brief definitions of what is meant by these three areas of strategy, marketing and teams.

Obsession One: business strategy

Strategy is about planning where you want to go while being aware of the business environment – making your own plans while taking into consideration the outside factors.

Part of strategy is deciding where you want to be in, say, three years' time, where you want to be in one year's time and, therefore, what it is that you need to do now. It is about deciding what race you want to win, against whom you wish to be racing, and deciding your definition of winning.

Strategy can be seen in terms of trade-offs. The essence of trade-offs is that you cannot always hedge your bets by betting on two horses. Sometimes you have to decide which horse to back. Trade-offs recognise that you need to decide what you want and what the consequences of that decision might be. For example, you cannot always go for two conflicting goals: a totally committed workforce and one that you can call on as and when you need them; you cannot usually command a high price for a low-quality item.

No one ever said that thinking strategically was easy and the textbooks don't help! But the clearer you are about what you are trying to do and the context of your efforts, then the easier it all becomes. The simpler your strategy, then the easier it is for your staff and your customers to understand what it is that you are trying to do. This focus and simplicity breeds success.

Obsession Two: marketing

Marketing is another misunderstood word in the business world. As with 'strategy', we use the word 'marketing' all over the place and give it different meanings depending upon our mood and our inclination. No wonder no one respects these words or the people who use them a lot.

The textbook definition is 'identifying and satisfying customer needs profitably', but this is a very academic definition and so may not be very helpful to those people running a business.

A better definition might be 'Marketing is about deciding what customers' business you want to win, against whom, and how.'

Marketing is seeing your business through your customers' eyes. What problem does your product or service solve? Why should people buy from you? What benefits are you offering that your competition doesn't offer? If you aren't offering additional benefits then why should people buy from you at all?

Your business leaks messages about itself like radioactivity. It is not possible not to communicate: everything you do communicates something. As that is the case, you should decide what it is that you wish to be communicating and be clear about whom you want to be communicating with and what the message is that you want them to receive.

In some senses marketing equals communication. Marketing is about systematically selecting how and what you communicate to whom, with the purpose of winning more of the business that you want.

Obsession Three: teams and people

Most businesses have some kind of 'people' problems. Psychologists (and comedians) would describe these as 'issues'!

It is inevitable that as the business grows there will be conflicting pressures at force: the pressure to get more business, the pressure to do more and more work of higher and higher quality, and the pressure to work together. Eventually these pressures lead to conflicts. The resolution of the conflicts requires compromise. It is likely that there will be casualties.

In fact, most business teams sow the seeds of their own destruction. The *raison d'être* of starting many businesses is to escape the inertia created by bureaucratic and systemised functional organisations. Ironically, most growing businesses require the very order and structure that they were created to escape.

Successful teamwork requires the ability to motivate, lead and communicate effectively. There are far too many examples of getting these skills wrong and not enough best-practice examples for us to talk about.

ACTION POINT

Right now, score your business! How obsessed are you? Take each heading (strategy, marketing, teams and people), and give your business a score out of ten (where 0 means that you pay the subject very little attention at all and 10 means that you are totally obsessed by the subject). In fact, while you are scoring your own business you might as well score your two main competitors, and the business you most admire. Score them as to how good you think they are according to the criteria. You don't need to be too scientific about this – the general scores will give you some insight into how you stand when put against them. Write down the scores in the book on the page.

So, here goes . . . mark your scores out of ten. Consider the various score distributions. In all honesty can you justify your scores? Where is the evidence to support your scores? What could you do to improve the scores? Mark for how obsessed your business is about the following:

Heading:	Your score	Competitor A	Competitor B	The 'best'
Strategy				
Marketing				
Teams				

Consider the following:

Regarding strategy:

- If you don't know where you are going, then any road will do!
- If you don't know where you are going, then how do you know how well you are progressing?
- If you don't know your competitors' strengths and weaknesses, then how do you hope to compete, and against what?

- If you are not aware of trends and pressures in the market and industry, then how do you expect to make the best, most rational decisions?

- To be constantly reacting to the moves of your competitors will grind you down – take control. It is usually better to be at the front, in the lead, than at the back of the pack (in a team of huskies, it is only the dogs at the front that have a good view!).

Regarding marketing, why should people buy from you if:

- You aren't able to give them what they want?
- You don't understand their needs and their wants?
- You aren't talking their language?
- Your competition is faster/smarter/nicer/cheaper?

Regarding teams and people, what will happen to your business, if:

- Your people are not communicating effectively?
- The different departments don't communicate properly?
- Staff keep leaving?
- Your people don't get on with each other?
- Your staff were really 'firing on all cylinders'?

Case study

Amanda Barry of award-winning Amanda Barry Communications (ABC) reminds us to take control of the business rather than let events control us – adversity forced her to refocus her efforts on strategy, marketing and teams.

'One of the big challenges faced by ABC has been moving away from a position of extreme vulnerability when we had one dominating major client. In 1998, almost 60 per cent of our business came from just one source. There was a large variety of projects from this one client, but we were still very exposed should the work dry up. Then the unthinkable happened and the client embarked on a rationalisation programme that meant cutting down its many PR consultancies to just one international agency and we were given notice.

'Even though we had anticipated this happening, it was still very difficult when we came face to face with the reality. However, it was the best thing that could have happened to us. We were forced to reassess our entire business and change our fundamental approach to winning new clients.

'New business was no longer a nice added extra – it was a vital part of our everyday survival. We had to sit down and look at what we were trying to achieve. We looked at what our competitors were doing and what out customers really wanted. Armed with this information, we were able to make some bold decisions about how we were going to develop the business.

'Our strategy for recruiting new employees also evolved. Although we didn't make anyone redundant during this difficult period, we did have to reassess our whole rationale when looking for new staff. Once, we had the luxury of taking on young, relatively inexperienced people and training them ourselves over a long period of time. Now, we had to look for associates who could play an active part in winning and managing new client business – from day one. We also began working with trusted freelancers who could help us manage the very busy periods, but not sit on our books through the quieter times.

'Now, eighteen months on, the business no longer relies on any one client but has a healthy mix of small to medium-size accounts, typically between 10 and 15 per cent of our income. We are once again in a period of growth and regularly pitch for and win new business. We can weather the loss of any one client when the project comes to an end without any serious consequences – it's just part of the ebb and flow of the business. The lesson has been a tough one, but one that ultimately means that ABC is a stronger, more resilient business because of it.'

Sounding off: why we choose to ignore these basics – just like dieting!

For some, the business's search for the holy grail often seems to be about looking for the latest management fad and seeing whether it can be applied to make the business any better. Just like diet programmes, most of the fads do not work – they are a con.

Good businesses are preoccupied with three basic things – they have the obsessive focus on teams and people, on marketing and what the customer wants, and on strategy and planning. All else is commentary. If these basics are not in place then the business will not be sustainable.

Frequently asked questions

Q. I've got a business to run! Isn't focusing on your so-called 'triad' a luxury?

A. You need to spend time working on tomorrow's business as well as working on today's. The triad (strategy, marketing and teams) is the obsession of the highly successful. Look at any business that is top of its class, and you will see this fixation in the way it behaves. It may not be deliberate or explicit but the obsessive behaviour will be there. It's your choice whether you wish to follow suit!

Q. The real basics are getting staff to work, getting products through the factory gates and collecting the cash – you don't even mention finance in your list – how can you ignore money?

A. Of course, finance is a business basic. That is not in dispute. However, there is a very powerful argument that says that even if your financial controls, systems and procedures are sorted, then financial success will still be the consequence of your activity in the fields of marketing and operations (remember FiMO). Excellent FiMO score results are seen as a consequence of a business being obsessed and passionate about the triad, this Holy Trinity.

Q. If it is as simple as you make out, why hasn't anyone told me?

A. I guess that many people like to complicate things when it is simply not necessary. There is a lot of research supporting the triad – sometimes the researchers find it difficult to hone down their years of research into one crisp sentence, but if they could they would say, 'The highly successful are obsessed with three things etc., etc. . . .'

Q. Where are these glorious examples of the 'successful'?

A. Smaller local businesses seem best able to maintain the triad. It seems that the institutionalisation created by the size of larger businesses dilutes their ability to focus consistently on the 'threesome'. If you want names that we all know that have demonstrated the 'beautiful obsession', then look no further than Virgin, Body Shop, Amazon, Easyjet, and Ben and Jerry's. There are good reasons why these businesses have caused such a stir and grown so quickly.

Q. So, which one should I focus on first – strategy, marketing or teams?

A. If only life were so simple! I think that the three are all inter-linked. You cannot separate them out into discrete, independent boxes. As you work on your future so you should be thinking about all three simultaneously.

Summary

The best businesses are focused on marketing, strategy and teams. Are you? How could you become more passionate, especially as the business grows and starts to become bureaucratic? How can you revitalise your business to put back the zest and excitement that the smaller, younger businesses so often seem to have?

CHAPTER THREE

Where do you want to go?

Vision, mission and purpose statements have fans and enemies – some clear indication or statement of direction is required because, if you don't know where you want to go, then any road will do! If your vision is to be taken seriously, then how do you create one that you really can believe in?

Many people belittle mission and vision statements, and they are often right to do so. Their presence in company reception areas and the contempt disillusioned employees give them have done them no end of harm. Quite right, really. The standard vision or mission statement normally reads something like this:

> We at Bloggs Incorporated seek to be a world-class provider of widgets to a specific industry. We seek co-operative partnerships with our staff and with our customers in order to deliver outstanding products and services while generating exceptional dividends to our shareholders while improving the environment and the local community.

These statements are banal and meaningless because no one really believes them, even if they remember or even understand what they really mean. However, just because previous attempts at these statements have not worked, it does not mean that there is no real value to be had from trying to state what it is that your business is trying to do. If you are able to start to define where you want to be and what you want to be, then you are also starting to define what it is that you do *not* want to be. This process of defining the direction that you wish to move in makes it easier to decide what the steps on the way will need to be.

The more focus you have, the greater your clarity, then the easier it is for you to define the path. And remember: if you do not know where you want to go then any road will do!

While many consultants get very excited about the definitions of purpose, vision, mission, objectives and goals, what really counts is how you can use the process to define and determine the future development of your business.

ACTION POINT

Right now, write down the answer to the following three questions. Spend at least five minutes answering each question.

> Where do you want the business to be in three years' time?
> So, where does the business *need* to be in a year's time?
> So, what do you need to be doing now?

Having attempted the questions above you can now start to flesh out your answers in a little more detail.

So far, specific definitions of mission and vision have been avoided. It would be useful to have some working definitions that will be used throughout the book. Academics often squabble about exact definitions. Rather than search for the final and absolute definitions of various terms, we will agree to use the following interrelated definitions.

> ■ Level One Goal or 'Business Vision': the 'blue skies' picture of what success would smell, taste, feel, and look like. The vision is the goal that you seek to attain, what you are trying to be – such as 'to be perceived as the best . . .', 'to be known as . . .', 'to be the best place to . . .', to be the only . . .'
> ■ Level Two Goal or 'Business Mission': the numbers that you will need to achieve in order to achieve the business vision – such as 'employing 50 staff', 'turning over £2 million per annum', 'to work with the ten key blue chip companies', 'making a net profit margin in excess of 15 per cent'.

What underpins the business vision and mission are two further concepts:

- Values: what is important to your business and how you conduct your business. Values are codes of conduct that you will not turn your back on – 'we are an eco-friendly organisation', 'nonsexist', '100 per cent trustworthy'.

- Purpose: focuses on why the business exists – 'to deliver remarkable attention to the dietary needs of the Jewish community', 'to inspire local children to play the piano', 'to build the best-value reproduction conservatories in the Greenwich area'.

Some people believe that the vision/mission/values/purpose 'trip' is purely self-congratulatory egocentric nonsense. Just because the way in which these 'statements' have been delivered has made them the laughing stock of many intelligent businesspeople, you should still not underestimate the power of the process of sorting out what your business really stands for.

The greater your clarity about what your business is trying to do, the easier it is to formulate and communicate your message to your team, your staff, your customers and even your suppliers. The business vision and mission are like a road map. They define your end point and hence they enable you to focus your efforts on that goal. The real power of a business comes when it is able to focus and concentrate all its efforts rather than dissipating that power.

Purpose and values inform you as to how you wish to travel that journey.

Case study

RCA Sound was a highly successful sound recording studio run by Rick in the 1990s. Because of a commitment to 'real sound' as opposed to electronic and synthesised sounds (he was going to set up a Campaign for Real Recording), the studio was clear about which work it would or would not accept. This is all about values. These values were the very reason for the business existing. Rick would not sacrifice his values by recording synthesised music and in the end this made his studio stand out from the rest.

Case study

Bert Clemens looked at the state of the North European pre-cooked-meals market and decided to be the leading Belgian producer of prepared precooked meals within three years. A bold vision, and yet he now supplies to supermarkets across all of Europe.

Case study

Gerry Bentley set up an executive mentoring and coaching business with a clear mission. 'In ten years' time, we will own and run ten offices in each of ten countries, employing a total of 100 consultants generating £10 million and a net profit of £1 million.' Absolute clarity here.

Is your vision a BHAG?

Visionary companies often use bold missions. These can also be called BHAGs, Big Hairy Audacious Goals, pronounced bee-hags. A BHAG is a powerful mechanism to stimulate progress. Most companies have goals, but there is a difference between merely having a goal and becoming committed to a huge, daunting challenge. The concept of the BHAG comes from Collins and Porras' *Built to Last*.

In the 1960s President Kennedy didn't have a goal to 'do a bit more in space'. Despite there being a less than 50:50 belief in getting a man on the moon, in 1961, he still declared that 'this nation shall commit itself to achieving the goal, before the decade is out, of landing a man on the moon and returning safely to Earth'. At the time this statement was outrageous. It was a BHAG, and what a BHAG does is provide a unifying focal point of effort, often creating immense team spirit.

A BHAG engages people – it reaches out and engages their emotions. It is tangible, energising and exciting, and it has a clear finish line. As the goal becomes the focal point, so the leader becomes less important.

BHAGs are particularly well suited to entrepreneurs and small companies.

- Sam Walton's BHAG was to make his first dime store the most successful in Arkansas within five years. (This is now Wal-Mart.)
- Tom Watson Sr's goal was to transform his tiny one-building company into the International Business Machines Corporation. (This is now IBM.)
- Sony set out to design, develop and sell a pocket radio.
- For many start-ups, to simply get up and survive is a pretty audacious goal.

Case study

Andy Gilbert runs a company called Go MAD, where MAD stands for 'Make A Difference'. The charity part of the business intends to show youngsters how to be more effective in their lives. Andy's BHAG is known as his rule of one in ten – he wants to reach one million youngsters in ten years. Not bad, eh?

Case study

KJ Printing Systems was a generalist printer with 75 employees. Margins on standard print jobs were ever decreasing. In recent years they focused on printing large advertisements for roadside hoardings. They decided that their future lay in investing in a unique technology for large-sized (photographic) printing. It was at this point that they still lacked clarity about the future and worked through the process of developing a BHAG. The results are below.

Core purpose

To make it hassle-free for advertisers and their agencies to get superb-quality print advertisements on their hoardings.

Core values

- Customer-led
- State-of-the-art technology
- Dedicated
- Professional
- Growing profit

BHAG

To create a reputation for quality and reliability such that 70 per cent of advertising agencies actually stipulate that they want KJ to print the advert. (Within three years.) To be known as the only printer worth working with. To be the leader in our class, proven by awards.

Vivid description

It is 2007. We are in the car park at KJ. There is a series of company cars ahead of us – convertible Saabs, the new BMW sports. We enter through the glass double door. The ground floor is a throng of activity. It is a high-ceilinged hallway that has hoardings adorning its walls. It is like a church dedicated to the art of tasteful persuasion. You would never know that behind this room dedicated to style is a printing works.

Young designers with portfolio cases are engaged in passionate conversation with our print managers. On the walls are some of the most memorable advertising hoardings of the last few years. All the famous and/or notorious brands have had their work printed by us: Benetton, Wonderbra, Coca-Cola. It's like a who's who of the classiest advertisers.

At reception a backlit glass cabinet houses some of the most prestigious awards of the industry. There are photos of the MD with Kate Moss (after 'that advert') and with Robbie Williams at the Golden Globe Awards.

The factory floor is a hive of activity, with the latest digital printing technology in evidence. Fifty men and women at work in what resembles a dust-free environment. In the finishing room we can see the last touches being put on our latest project – the McDonald's hologram advert for the opening event at the forthcoming Olympics. Another coup for KJ.

The design studio comprises thirty designers working at computers – there is bustle, there is excitement, and the phones are ringing. Controlled chaos. The sales and administration floor is relaxed, informal yet with an air of success. All areas are clean and tidy. The style is very Scandinavian – large plants, large windows, and wonderful views of the countryside.

The works canteen is very Ikea! Meetings are going on here rather than in a boardroom. This is a place where people are happy to be working.

ACTION POINT

Go back to your original vision and ask yourself if it is compelling enough. Do you have a Big Hairy Audacious Goal or do you have dull, uninspiring goals like 'do better than last year'? Where's the passion and excitement in that? Rewrite your vision until it is a BHAG – this in turn will inspire you to rewrite your mission and will affect your strategy.

Step One – What is your core purpose?
Step Two – What are your core values?
Step Three – What is your Big Hairy Audacious Goal (BHAG)?
Step Four – Write a vivid description of your BHAG.

Checklist – BHAG

- [ ] Is it clear?
- [ ] Is it compelling?
- [ ] Does it require little explanation? It shouldn't.
- [ ] Is it a goal (rather than a statement)?
- [ ] Does it get people's juices going?
- [ ] Is it outside the comfort zone? It should be.
- [ ] Does it have a life of its own beyond the leader?
- [ ] Is it consistent with the company's beliefs and ideologies?

Case study

Ross Kinneir talks about his business:

Kinneir Dufort is a niche-market, hi-tech product-design and prototyping consultancy. After twenty years of modest growth and being patted on the back and talked down to by the bank, and being told that of course they would support us when the time was right, I got a call from a young girl doing telephone marketing.

'Good afternoon. My name is Louise calling from XYZ Bank and I wondered whether you need any business finance.' Without pausing I said, 'Yes, actually, we shall be needing half a million next week if you could get someone to call me back.'

I thought, 'Well now we might unlock the riddle of how we move on and up'. Our problem was premises because we did not want to move to rented space and spend money doing up someone else's property – we wanted to sell our little studio and buy big. There was pressure building up for things to happen in our twelve-strong team. So I phoned other banks. The response was electric. Very soon we had written mortgage offers from several.

It felt just like coastal fresh air. Our frustrated and pent-up need converted into a fast-moving action plan. We bought an empty ten-thousand-feet sugar refinery/warehouse in central Bristol. We mobilised architect and builders. We explained the whole project to our Kinneir Dufort team – they had to be enthused and convinced we were doing the right thing for them as well. It caused very serious distraction from ongoing consultancy – being perfectionists is not easy, particularly in new territory.

We told clients what we were planning. 'So, um, you're moving to a posh, city-centre, converted warehouse? Nice, but we don't like the prospect of increased fees.'

Ten months later we moved in. The accountants' spreadsheets had shown that even if we did not grow we could afford the mortgage repayments. Well that turned out to be just a partial truth. There was no going back. We have a prestigious building – five times the size of the old one.

The result is very rewarding. Clients love it here. The team has trebled in three years – far quicker and easier than we ever imagined. We are already starting a second major expansion – raising the roof to grow to 45 people.

We are now more profitable than before; the future looks more secure; we are taking on more team members because we have the space and we can generate the commissions. We are working in Europe, Scandinavia, USA and Japan. We are investing in further serious computerised design and prototyping facilities.

I remember an earlier accountant saying that I was wrong to have bought the first little coach-house premises (before I even bought a house): 'You are a designer – not a property company. Concentrate all your efforts and investment in design.' He had not seen the formula the same way as us. For the Kinneir Dufort design team, the right premises are crucial to success. It's not a mystery: we need a unique combination of studios, machine workshops, offices, meeting rooms and parking, all with the right ambience to make both us and our clients feel good about business.

The moral of this story is – talk to more people about what might be possible, and combine it with what your talents and ambition tells you. Do challenge the norm, and do expect to be taken seriously. Don't wait for the call – make it.

– Ross Kinneir

Frequently asked questions

Q. Most visions are empty and meaningless. How can I make ours any different?

A. Most visions are written by committees or by outsiders, so they have no real value. It is well worthwhile to gather your team together and work out as a group what it is that you do and what it is that you aspire to do and what would be your BHAG. A BHAG will influence the rest of the strategy and planning processes. People spend a lot of time at work and would prefer to be part of something that they believe in and can belong to.

Q. Do we have to parade our BHAG at reception?

A. The BHAG is essentially for internal, staff use. It can be shown off if you feel that it is appropriate. It is often better to expose goals that you will achieve: for instance, budgets should be based on the shorter-term realistic goals. Keep your true ambitions hidden from the cynics, as they will relish the opportunity to mock any of your shortcomings.

Q. How do I make this vision thing work for the business?

A. The most important thing about your vision is that you believe in it. If you don't believe in it then it probably won't happen. Get key people in the business to start talking about what you are in business to achieve. The discussion will help you to establish what you want and what you don't want. It will be an opportunity for you to demonstrate your leadership skills and give them an opportunity to lift their view up beyond day-to-day issues.

Summary

Do you know where you want to be in, say, three or five years' time? Do you know what success would smell like? What is it that you are trying to achieve and why? You must be clear about what you want the business to achieve, because without goals you cannot motivate yourself or measure your progress.

Following on, you need to measure your capabilities and opportunities, which are referred to as the strategy workout – this enables you to understand the various options that are available to the company. If you get the workout sorted, then you are able to get the planning and the vision aligned.

CHAPTER FOUR

Strategic thinking

This is an introduction to strategic thinking – that is, thinking about strategy in a way that can help your business. Let's be clear that strategy is simply about planning while being aware of the outside. This chapter examines what strategy is, and it looks at the different issues that you need to consider when formulating a workable strategy for your business. This chapter should be read while starting to consider the sessions in Part Two, which will help you to understand the context of your business.

'Failing to plan is planning to fail.'

– Brian Tracy

'More than ever, I am persuaded that it is not the insides of organisations that ought to be preoccupying the boards of directors, but the outsides, because the outsides are changing so fast and so momentously.'

– Charles Handy

What is strategy?

Strategy is . . .

> ■ Planning, while being aware of the outside environment
> ■ The pattern of decisions that intentionally or otherwise sets the long-term direction of the company and determines its fate – deciding which race you want to win (against whom)

And so a superior strategy must equal a different strategy – a strategy that is different from that of your competitors.

In the words of the management professor Peter Drucker, 'Whenever you see a successful company, someone has made a courageous decision.' Successful businesspeople make courageous decisions. Profit and risk go hand in hand.

All competitors who persist over time must maintain a unique advantage by being different from the rest. Managing that difference is the essence of long-term business strategy. It is not enough to be different from the rest: your customers must recognise and value that difference.

Harvard Business School's Professor Ken Ohmae said, 'It will make for clearer thinking if we reserve the term strategy for actions aimed directly at altering the strength of the enterprise relative to that of the competitors.' He has focused on the essence of strategy: you must make your decisions in a competitive environment.

The final quotation comes from Professor Michael Porter, who said, 'Competitive strategy is about being different. It means deliberately choosing a different set of activities to deliver a unique mix of value . . . The essence of strategy is in choosing what not to do. Without trade-offs there would be no need for choice and thus no need for strategy.' While Porter's work has sometimes been difficult to apply to a real business, his words on strategy are excellent.

Strategy and your business

Strategy, to my mind, is the plan to get *there* and establishing where *there* is (while being aware of the outside environment!).

Your business needs to know where it wants to be in five years' time. If you know where you want to be in five years' time, then it becomes self-evident where you need to be in a year's time. The issue, then, is whether you have got the capability and whether there are the opportunities available to achieve these goals. If the answer is positive, then you proceed with the business plan.

So, strategic business planning is based upon several key tenets:

- Vision and mission
- The business environment audit, and our capabilities and the opportunities available
- Planning to get there

First, do you know where you want to be in, say, five years' time? In faster-moving industries, such as computing, this time span may be considerably shorter. However, the question remains: do you know what success would smell like? What is it that you are trying to achieve?

The second key tenet is the necessity to measure capabilities and opportunities, which are loosely referred to as the business environment audit or the strategy workout. It is this stage in the process that really enables you to understand the various options that are available to the company. If you get the business environment audit right, then you are able to get the planning and the vision aligned.

The final tenet, the business plan, is the part that many organisations omit to complete. Planning is central to the achievement of goals. Success does not just happen, and crystallising your thoughts on paper may well save a lot of pain at later stages of a project.

Strategic business planning: a common-sense approach

This would be an appropriate place to quote the following Kipling verse:

> *I keep six honest serving men*
> *(They taught me all I knew);*
> *Their names are What and Why and When,*
> *And How and Where and Who.*

Remember the 'five Ws and an H'.

An audit of your business environment is a key tool in the drive to understand what options are available to the business. While business-school hype prefers impressive-sounding models for assessing the business environment, it is better to conduct your audit by asking the following questions, the 'business environment audit'. The audit is like peeling away the layers of an onion to get nearer and nearer its core and centre.

1 What drives the *industry*?
2 What drives the *market*?

3   Who are your *competitors*?
4   Who are your *customers*?
5   How do your *target customer groups* behave?
6   How good are you, *yourselves*?
7   What are your *capabilities and opportunities*?

These questions will be addressed one at a time.

1. What drives the industry, the market environment?

When looking at what drives the industry that a business is in, you can carry out the so-called PEST analysis. The PEST analysis addresses the following issues that may affect the business:

> ■ **Political issues.** These may include government changes, local political influences and mood. For example, new environmental or local government legislation may create new opportunities to private waste companies.
>
> ■ **Economic issues.** These could include currency exchange rates, terms of trade, trade barriers, 'feel-good' factors and interest rates. For example, exchange rates are crucial to a local wine importer.
>
> ■ **Sociological issues.** These reflect the sociocultural mood, such as swings towards consumerism, out-of-town shopping, increased crime, levels of education or poverty. For instance, local retail outlets suffer severe competition from big out-of-town multiples.
>
> ■ **Technological issues**. These may include information technology, cheaper travel, use of mobile phones, and the 'communication revolution'. For example, the mobile-phone industry is a relatively recent and very fast-moving industry to enter.

The PEST analysis gives us a good idea of the climate and key issues that might be confronted by all businesses in a particular industry. By looking at these factors, you can start to assess how these outside factors could influence you and your competition. If you are fortunate, you will be able to take advantage of your awareness of these factors (see Part Two, Session Five).

2. What drives the market?

You should now take the market for your goods and services, and ask the following questions:

- ☐ Who are the key players in the market (today and tomorrow)?
- ☐ What determines the nature of the market?
- ☐ What are the trends and benchmarks of performance within the market?
- ☐ What are the key influences on the market? For example:
  - ☐ Marketing spend
  - ☐ Pricing policy
  - ☐ How prices are set
  - ☐ Size of the market
  - ☐ Location
  - ☐ Complements, e.g. the price of things that go with your product affects demand for your product (cars and petrol, computers and printers)
  - ☐ Substitutes, e.g. the price of things that can replace your product (train travel for car travel, taxis for buses)
  - ☐ Barriers to entry, e.g. do start-up costs, knowledge and resources required create a barrier to prevent others from entering your industry?

The better an understanding you have of the market, the better your chance of predicting how it will develop. Often it is useful to draw comparisons between your own market and one that demonstrates, or has demonstrated, similar trends.

As an example, there are tremendous similarities between the way in which vinyl records have tried to fight off competition and ultimately failed (from audio tape and then compact disc and then digital audio tape) and the way in which the gas industry fought off the development of the electricity industry. Likewise, the same is true of the revamps of the old roller skate, as it becomes the roller boot, in-line skate, snake-skate and so forth. In marketing terms, this is referred to as revitalising the product's life cycle. (See Part Two, Sessions Six and Eight.)

3. Who are your competitors?

Be clear about whom you are competing with and what their strengths, weaknesses, opportunities and threats are. If you know, for instance, what your key competitors face in terms of overheads, staff costs and their cash situation, then you can try to second-guess how they are thinking about the market. This kind of information is often relatively easy to obtain, although sometimes a little detective work is necessary. Company brochures, coupled with annual reports and/or company records from one of the annual-report databases, give information that gives a real insight.

An even more fundamental question than 'Who are your competitors today?' is, 'Who will be your competitors tomorrow?' If you intend to be in business tomorrow, then you must do your best to establish exactly whom you will be competing against and what exactly is their profile. In other words, what are their strengths, weaknesses, opportunities and threats? If you can understand where your competitors are coming from and what they are trying to achieve, then maybe you can take measures to counteract or pre-empt any moves that they might make. It's all a bit like a game of chess!

The same questions need to be asked, time and time again, to develop an insight into exactly how your competitors might behave:

- Who are they?
- What are they trying to achieve in the short run? In the long run?
- What will their next move be?
- What are their strengths?
- What is their Unique Selling Proposition (USP)?
- When will they make their next move?
- How do other competitors perceive them?
- Who are their customers?
- Why have they got them?
- How do the customers perceive them?
- Where are they competing?
- Where are they trying to get?

(See Part Two, Session Seven.)

4. Who are your customers?

Customers are fickle and you need to understand how, why and when your customers buy. The better you are able to understand their buying habits, then the better you are able to satisfy their needs. You need to get as close as possible to your customers.

When you look at who your customers are, just as with the competitors, you need to know who they are not only today, but also tomorrow. The reasons why people are your customers, or used to be, will provide valuable information about what you are doing right, and what you are doing wrong.

One excellent question and one that sits at the core of marketing, is, 'Who do you want your customers to be?' If you know whom it is that you should be selling to, then you have come a long way towards 'segmenting' your market.

Modern marketing is about developing long-term relationships, where possible, with your customers. The closer you are to your customers, the greater advantage you have over your competitors in terms of satisfying customer needs.

Again, you can use the Rudyard Kipling's 'five Ws and an H':

- [ ] Why do they buy the product and/or service?
- [ ] Why do they buy from us?
- [ ] Why do they leave us?
- [ ] What stops them from buying more?
- [ ] When do they buy?
- [ ] How do they use the product and/or service?
- [ ] How do they buy?
- [ ] How often do they buy?
- [ ] Where do they buy?
- [ ] Who does the buying?
- [ ] Who uses the product and/or service?
- [ ] Who are your customers?

5. How do your target customer groups behave?

Customer groups or 'target market segments' are certainly what traditional marketers get very excited about. The crux of marketing is segmentation (of your market) and differentiation (of your product offering). In layman's terms, segmentation means dividing the customers into different groups according to shared characteristics (age, sex, buying habits, geography). Differentiation is about making yourself appear to be different from the rest (in the eyes of the customer).

With the notion of segmenting (that is, dividing up) your market comes the opportunity to focus on the needs and buying habits of individual groups. The beauty of segmentation – and, more specifically, having distinct customer groups that you are aiming at (your Target Market Segment, TMS) – is that you can focus your attention on how and when and where these people buy your particular product. You end up focusing your offering in response to the needs of the particular audience. And with focus comes effectiveness and increased sales and profit.

Target customer grouping will also make you think about how your product offering, or brand, is perceived by the customer groups. In other words, how are you positioned? Are you a market leader, or follower, or niche player, or what?

Target customer grouping is also about understanding what makes that particular grouping or segment 'tick'. What makes the group change its buying behaviour? What things influence it?

(See Part Two, Session Fourteen.)

6. How good are you, yourselves?

Last, but by no means least, you have to take a long, cool look at your own organisation and yourselves. After you have looked at the environment in which you are competing, you must evaluate just how good you really are. This is no easy task.

The real art in strategic thinking is to be able to get an accurate perspective on your own organisation.

- What are your weaknesses?
- What are your opportunities?
- What are your threats?
- What are your strengths?
- How good are you, really?

Use the tools outlined in Chapter One on FiMO and RECoIL to evaluate yourselves. Not only do you need to understand just how good and appropriate your own organisation is for the task ahead, but you also need to understand how you are perceived by your customers and by your competitors. All this will start to fill in the picture so that you can get a full, clear and reasonably objective view of what is going on. Again, do not hold back on those 'five Ws and an H' questions:

- Who are your customers?
- Why do they buy from you?
- Where does your reputation come from?
- Why do you have this reputation?
- What are you trying to say to the market?
- What do they think they are buying when they buy from you?
- Who else would they buy from?
- How do your customers see you?
- How do your competitors see you?
- When do they buy from you?

(See Part Two, Session One.)

7. What are your capabilities and opportunities?

If you put together the six stages above and apply the FiMO/RECOIL framework from Chapter One, you should have a pretty clear idea of what your capabilities are and also what your opportunities are.

This task, like many in management, is much easier to say than to do. I would not for one minute pretend that this is an easy task; but, the more information you have, the clearer the various trends become.

> 'In strategy it is important to see distant things as if they were close and to take a distanced view of close things'
> – *Miyamoto Musashi, Kendo Master, 1645*

Case study

Antonia Graham's Graham and Green went on a business growth training programme in London. Learning about strategy and, as important, learning how to make it happen, changed Antonia's attitude to planning and the day-to-day matters.

'My mind is more focused and more vigorous and the future of the business has gone from rather misty to very clear Technicolor. I try to get everyone to do something important every day and not get bogged down in the little details. You've got to take regular steps towards the goals.'

Case study

Business Systems UK supply niche market support products around a telephony environment. They have never had trouble growing. In ten years, they developed from two men in an office selling a product they believed in, into a hugely successful business with a staff of sixty and a turnover of £10 million per annum.

The founders, Stephen and Richard, realised that their business was not only growing, but was changing. A new range of skills would be needed to take them into the future they wanted for the business. Stephen Thurston explains:

'There are stages in a business's growth when it starts feeling and behaving like a totally different animal, and that's what prompted us to look for assistance.

'We learned about two painful stages of growth. We were growing so fast that we didn't notice the first one (which typically happens at about the £1–2 million per annum turnover mark), but there is another at around £8–9 million where you hit a brick wall and growth tends to stall. We knew that we would have to devolve control of the company if we intended to meet our aggressive growth plans. You must start with the end in mind, and work backwards from that. You break the goal down into targets. Then you have to think, What's the product mix got to be to support this growth? What skills do we need to drive us in that direction?'

Case study

Sally Carrick of Carrick Travel tells how her business has had to adapt to survive. A keen eye on the competition and a keen eye on her customers plus sheer determination in a cut-throat industry are some of her traits. Let's look further.

Background

Carrick Travel Limited, established in 1974 in Kenilworth, Warwickshire. Now has a staff of fifty, including some part-timers, and a turnover of £11 million. Retail travel agent with five branches. Tour operating, distributing through own retail offices, media and website.

Specialist areas include cruising, golf, escorted group tours and overseas conference and incentive travel. Founded by two enthusiastic travellers, Sally and Mike Carrick, who previously had worked for multiple travel agencies but were not enamoured with the lack of in-depth knowledge of travel agencies in general.

First milestone: About five years down the line – realisation that all agencies had the same suppliers and sold the same products. We needed to specialise and bring in expertise. First additional director appointed, who created the Carrick Tours programme, which offered 'tailor-made' individual and group itineraries with unusual destinations. These programmes developed and included the first commercial flight of Concorde into Birmingham Airport as well as a bespoke Carrick America programme. Opening of additional retail offices in Leamington Spa and Coventry.

Late 1980s

Challenges: Major travel agencies bought up by tour operators, e.g. Thomson's had bought Lunn Poly and were increasing the number of shops dramatically. Vertically integrated companies established with more favourable commercial terms given to their own shops. Commencement of the discount dilemma – massive discounts ostensibly offered by the vertically integrated companies. Nervous reaction from the independent travel agencies (e.g., Carrick Travel). We came up with the free taxi ride to the airport, free insurance, tactical discount campaigns. End result – two or three years of nil growth but managed to retain a profit.

Decision: Not to discount but improve sales with a better-informed and intelligent service. Embarked on an intensive and ongoing staff training programme. Concentrated on gaining PR for your local agency who offer impartial advice.

1990s

Challenges: Competition intensifies from the major suppliers as they buy up the small independent tour operators and reduce their commercial terms and impose unrealistic targets (as the goal posts had moved).

Decision: Join a consortium of travel agents in order to gain improved commissions and better trading terms. Sally Carrick is now a director of the consortium of 220+ agents – a consortium that is still the only independent consortium not aligned to any tour operator.

Discussions: regarding other areas of business, decide to formalise a link-up with another company who specialise in conference venue finding in the UK and event management. This division is now the most profitable of Carrick Travel but we do share the profits 50/50 with the other company, who are responsible for sales.

Late 1990s

Challenges: Direct-sell telephone numbers on all pages of major suppliers. Breakdown of operator–agent relationship as clients encouraged to book direct and are offered the travel agency commission. Huge increase in the method of distribution of tour-operator products, e.g. coupons, labels, special consumer offers through newspapers etc. Low-cost airlines. Internet bookings and dotcom companies offloading surplus stock. Discounts offered directly to our clients while in resorts.

Decisions: Appointment of additional director. Establishment of Carrick Travel website – higher cost of investment than envisaged but will continue. Charge clients for use of credit cards (in line with other agencies). Refurbishment of the Carrick offices to modernise and streamline.

Computerisation of all offices – recognising need to improve the database and improve relationship marketing (ongoing).

Appointment of marketing manager but this appointment was unsuccessful now decided to outsource.

Future

In view of impending cap on commissions by airlines, development of management fee structure for business travel and recognising the need to charge administration fees on certain transactions – new culture for older members of staff.

More specialised areas of business. Cruising specialist appointment made. Tailor-made itineraries by appointment. Australasia division established. Development of the overseas conference division. Invest more on the image of the company to differentiate Carrick Travel from the average travel agent.

Conclusions: Determination to overcome our need to depend on major suppliers. Do more of our own thing but be aware of the profit margins available in travel. Work closely with the Internet and sell it as a service along with own products. Raise profile in public's eye of Carrick Travel and offer ourselves as 'The Traveller's Travel Agent', offering impartial advice and recognising that the travel agent is the product.

Checklist – possible threats

- Could newcomers create damaging competition?
- Could a rival technology or newcomer overtake you?
- Is the market developing in ways that favour the competition?
- Could your customers become competitors?
- Is there a major area in the market where you lag?
- Could an unsuspected threat arrive from outside the industry?

Frequently asked questions

Q. Who should be doing our strategy?

A. Strategy is the job of the senior management team that is leading the business. After all, if you don't know where you are going then any road will do!

Q. How often should you do strategy?

A. Most businesses need to take a cold hard look at their business at least once a year. Spend a day or so evaluating your business and the business environment. Be honest with yourselves and plan the way forward.

Q. We've written hundreds of strategies but we never stick to them. What can we do?

A. Part of a good strategy is the plan to actually put them into practice. Tools such as the Balanced Business Scorecard are ideal for putting your strategy into practice. Keep your strategies simple and make them easily understood by all. The one-page business plan is another ideal tool for this process.

Q. Can you give me a Ten Steps or Idiot's Guide to Strategy?

A. Use the worksheets in Part Two to look at your business and its business environment. It will ask the questions and help you understand the environment that your business is currently being affected by. As a result of the analysis, you will be able to select strategies that will help you to decide your way forward.

Q. How do I know if it is a good strategy?

A. Most good strategies are simple and easily understood. They give you an advantage over your competition as well as demonstrate value to your customers. Strategic business planning is about deciding what you want and planning towards achieving it.

Summary

Strategy is all about knowing what you do and what you don't do! Strategy is about deciding which race you want to run. Strategy is about being different from the rest of your competition. After all, if you are the same as the rest, then why should customers want to come to your business?

CHAPTER FIVE

Strategy, shmategy – a discussion on approaching strategy

This chapter discusses your approach to strategy – if you are impatient, skip the chapter and go straight to the worksheets in Part Two. 'Strategy' is one of the most overused and yet misunderstood words in business. As a result, managers and consultants have struggled to 'do' it properly. Many people have difficulties when they focus on strategy and strategic thinking; here we provide guidelines to overcome these problems, including the Smart Strategy Tool for writing fast strategies.

Strategy is a subject that people like to refer to, but often they don't really know what they mean by the word. We should not be surprised that many people find it difficult to actually think strategically when they are unclear about what strategy is all about.

Commonly asked questions include:

- Does our company have a strategy? Is it the right one?
- What exactly do we mean by a strategy?
- How should we go about designing our strategy?

Before talking about the actual 'doing' of strategy, let's be clear about some of the 'strategy' issues, and why strategy can go wrong. There is a requirement to do things in a different way from the old way. After all, if you keep doing what you have always done, then you will keep getting the same (not better) results; and to expect a different result from doing the same thing is a definition of insanity!

The problem

The main complaints about the strategy process are:

- There is little agreement about what strategy actually is and what it does.

- It gets lost, unco-ordinated, frustrating, messy and unfinished – there is lack of focus and clarity.

- Most people involved either question their own ability to contribute or arrogantly dominate and suffocate the process.

- No SMART goals are achieved (SMART is an acronym that is used to remind us that goals should be specific, measurable, attainable, realistic, time-based).

- Fear of the future, combined with fear of failure, makes the team behave like reindeer freezing on the road when blinded by the headlights of the oncoming lorry.

- Management 'speaking in tongues' and parading this as science – the tools are not helpful: they are superficial, confusing and too theoretical.

In a nutshell there are three reasons why strategy does not work.

1. Types of strategic thinking

Managers often fail to differentiate between business-unit strategy and what is referred to as 'corporate-centre' strategy. The reason for this is that business schools and consultants normally talk about big-business/corporate-centre strategy when they are talking about strategy.

Business-unit strategy is for single-product/market players or 'strategic business units' of conglomerates; corporate-centre strategy is for conglomerates that are planning the future and the relationships between the centre and its various subsidiaries. The distinction is crucial – this is where so much of the confusion comes from.

To misquote Orwell, 'Business-unit strategy, good; corporate-centre strategy, bad'.

Business-unit strategy, good – it gives you insights into where and how you need to do things differently. It helps you to see the business through the customers' and through the competitors' eyes. Both today and tomorrow. It shows you your strengths and weaknesses and where and how you should be expending your efforts. We will come back to this later.

There are instances where corporate-centre strategy is beneficial. Examples include where there are global economies of scale, brand benefits, regional or global economies of scale, overcoming technological barriers and so forth. You need only to think of Apple, Coca-Cola, Microsoft, Sony and Toshiba. But this type of thinking is pretty irrelevant if you are running your own business, or a business unit employing, say, 500 people

Moreover, for the multinational or conglomerate, the ability of the centre to generate strategies that have little to do with the needs of specific business units is awesome. Couple this with the centre's (and the board's) lack of contact with the territories and you can see the potential for disastrous decisions. Corporate strategies constantly frustrate and bamboozle the managers of regional business units.

2. No clarity of purpose

Put simply, business strategy is planning while being aware of the business environment. So, who should be involved? Consultants? The senior team? The whole team? Well, this depends on the level (and size) of the organisation that you are talking about.

Strategic thinking is not the same as strategic planning. In fact, strategic planning is an oxymoron (a combination of contradictory ideas) like 'friendly fire', 'fun run' or 'fighting for peace' – planning and thinking are totally different activities requiring different skills. Strategic thinking is the role of the strategy team – those beneath them should carry out the (strategic) planning.

Strategic thinking must be used to improve understanding of the environment and the options available to the business. Any analysis must help the decision-making process. There is no room for using models that are simply intellectually attractive. The task at hand is to shed light on options and directions and find evidence to support decisions about the future.

3. The use of tools and theories

At the business-unit level, the tools of analysis are relatively straightforward. The only real barriers to a successful strategy are intimidation by the so-called 'professionals' and their jargon. Rogue management consultants have been known to blind their clients with science: BCG matrices, Value Chain Analyses and differential equations bully the innocent client into agreeing to a strategy that they may not fully understand or appreciate but are too timid to admit their ignorance. Despite this, the manager may well understand their business and industry with a clarity and perspective that the models are unable to detect.

It is most notably at the corporate-centre level that the jargon takes over and so often the process turns into Frankenstein's monster – you have a much more sophisticated list of tools (product-portfolio analyses, discounted cash flow, matrices, three-dimensional modelling). A whole industry has grown up around corporate strategy – it is here that the business-school hype runs amok – 'Long live the emperor and his new clothes!'

More complex is almost always worse, and yet the corporate centre has a propensity to complicate things!

Most of the models of analysis, some good and some bad, are over thirty years old; few people in business honestly know how to use them effectively and appropriately. For today's entrepreneurial business, the relevance and value of the models must be questioned.

The solution

In order to work, the whole strategy process must be effective and practical. Highfalutin theory is not the order of the day! Participants need to start the process with no axes to grind.

Strategy can be likened to 'seeing': seeing behind, above, below, beyond, beside, ahead and through the future. To be effective, strategic thinking tools must satisfy the following conditions:

1   Reflect the business needs of today and tomorrow
2   Start with the customers – be rooted and immersed in market understanding

3 Be practical (not theoretical)
4 Be specific (not superficial)
5 Encourage a longer-term view
6 Be measurable

So ... who should be developing your strategy?

The right people rarely work on strategy development.

For business-unit strategy, each of the operating managers should be involved; for corporate-centre strategy, the chairman, CEO and a few close colleagues should be involved. In both instances, a cross-section of operational managers should be involved to influence, double-check and approve the thinking process.

The next-best solution is to involve a firm of management consultants. You must choose carefully, otherwise they will bring over-complex tools and theories. You need to be able to stop them from doing that by giving them a clear brief of what you want. A good relationship will pay dividends, as they can facilitate the process or give you the right tools to work out the way forward.

Where to start? A philosophical debate

If strategic thinking is a creative process then the best place to start is with where you would like to be, and work backwards to where you are now. Then you can work out how to get there (the BHAG school of thought).

If strategic thinking is a systematic, analytical process, then start with where you are now and work out where you think you can get to. The snag with this second approach is that constant use of linear thinking stifles your creativity. If you believe that 10 per cent growth in sales is realistic, then you will plan away the idea of faster growth and the need for more unusual approaches to achieve a truly stretching goal.

In reality, you need to combine both approaches.

How to do strategy – at the business-unit level

You need to know what target market groups (segments) you work in and how profitable they really are. Only then can you focus on what you do effectively and cut out the deadwood.

These are the crucial questions that you need to be able to answer:

- What business are you in? This question is not as straightforward as it appears – what business do your customers and competitors believe you to be in? And what do you believe your business to be? Manchester United is no longer just a football team; indeed, the merchandise side of the business means that branding is more important than ever. Starbucks is not simply selling coffee: it is selling an attitude to life.

- Where do you make the money? What parts of your organisation contribute the most value to the whole? Where is the real value being added? What parts of the industry generate the highest profits? This follows on to a series of external issues:
  - How good are your competitive positions?
  - Is this a good industry to be in?
  - What do your customers think about you, your product and the market?
  - What do your competitors think about you, your product and the market?

The external analysis can be followed by internal analysis so that you can establish:

- How do you raise profits quickly?
- How do you build long-term value?

How to do strategy – at the corporate-centre level

While this book is not aimed at the big corporations, it is useful for readers who work in them to be clear that corporate-centre strategy is flawed because the centre rarely represents or reflects the needs of the outposts. The centre has a life of its own. Few corporate centres are small. Most do not add enough value to justify their cost. Most destroy more value than they add.

Corporate-centre strategy must be approached with a great deal of scepticism and caution.

Checklist – strategic thinking

☐ Be clear about what you want to achieve from the strategy process. Is it business-unit or corporate-centre strategy that you are working on?

☐ Decide your goals and be prepared to pay the price – after all strategy, by definition, is about trade-offs.

☐ Do not undertake 'strategisation' unless a system is in place that allows strategy implementation – otherwise the whole process is counterproductive.

It is imperative that the strategy process is not seen in isolation of other processes. Strategy is not a 'black box', a one-off activity, carried out at annual awaydays – to think strategically is an art form.

The Smart Strategy Tool

To counter the usually laborious process of trying to gather data and create a strategy, you can use the 'Smart Strategy Tool' based on an idea from the business writer David Maister.

This approach to strategy does not waste a lot of time talking about your objectives and the current and future environment. It goes right to the heart of strategy for the short term – the things that really matter. It goes directly for actions and specifics and focuses on what is achievable and realisable and things that you can do something about now!

The Smart Strategy Tool focuses on four key business objectives:

☐ For shareholders – improving margins and profitability
☐ For sales – get better customers and sales

☐ For operations – improving productivity and staff skills
☐ For growth – innovation and building capability

ACTION POINT

A sheet is taken to review each of the areas above and SMART goals need to be achieved. In other words, the strategies must be specific, measurable, attainable, realistic, time-based. Put specific actions in the sheets – things that can be achieved and measured; no ambiguous phrases here. Take, say, half an hour on this task.

1 For financials/shareholders – improving margins and profitability				
Action	Person responsible	Time needed	Due date	How we know it's been done

2 For sales – getting better customers and sales				
Action	Person responsible	Time needed	Due date	How we know it's been done

3 For operations – improving productivity and staff skills				
Action	Person responsible	Time needed	Due date	How we know it's been done

4 For growth – innovation and capability building				
Action	Person responsible	Time needed	Due date	How we know it's been done

Summary

Working on your strategy is not so very difficult if you focus on understanding what you are trying to achieve. Do not get confused by the way that some parties have tried to make strategy sound highly convoluted and highly complicated. You can do it – and now!

CHAPTER SIX

Marketing

If marketing is so important, then why is it that so few people really understand what it is and how to do it? It is time to get back to basics. First, a quick explanation of why marketers have been so bad at marketing marketing! And then, the sort of issues that a bright marketing approach will ask of your business.

Many people take it for granted that if their business is thriving then they must be doing a good job at marketing it. All too often this assumption has disguised a lack of basic marketing skills. I think that some people have taken their eye off the ball while the latest sexy fad (quality, Internet) has swept us by. So, fads aside, what has been going on?

Why aren't growing firms all avid marketers?

First, marketing is often confused with selling, but they are very different animals. If the purpose of business is to get and keep a customer, then marketing is about deciding what you should do to achieve that purpose. In other words, marketing is about developing products or services that will satisfy customer wants. Selling, on the other hand, is simply about getting people to buy your product.

Second, marketing often seems to be made so complicated. Textbooks are full of high-flying theories appropriate for MBA programmes and brand managers of multinational companies. The average growing business, however, needs only a simple, yet powerful, toolkit to apply to its activities.

Global marketing strategy, as taught to MBAs, is very intellectually attractive but limited in its effectiveness for the average entrepreneur! Given that marketing is often misunderstood, and that it is not always communicated effectively for the growing business, what can you do about it?

Use common sense! Marketing is about knowing who you want your customers to be today and tomorrow; it is about understanding who your competitors are, today and tomorrow; it is about knowing what is going on in the marketplace and in the industry.

A report, *Marketing Success in Fast Growth SMEs* (by David Storey of Warwick Business School), is based on a series of fascinating case studies of 'live' businesses. Out of the research are drawn nine fundamental lessons:

1 **Use professional advice:** An outside professional can act as the catalyst to focus the business on to the importance of marketing.

2 **Use basic techniques:** Simple, basic techniques are what are required. Segmenting the market or using existing information more effectively may be all you need.

3 **Focus on the customer:** If you do this you will be better able to give the customer what they really want!

4 **Plan:** The discipline of putting the customer first brings with it systematic planning, prioritising and measuring effectiveness, all of which help business performance.

5 **A shift of focus changes other factors:** Focusing on customer needs changes the whole outlook of the business as it reviews all its functions in the new light.

6 **New rules create new markets:** New legislation, rules and regulations have created new opportunities for those actively seeking them.

7 **Get a competitive advantage:** By focusing on customer needs and marketing issues, businesses are able to establish a competitive advantage, as they are able to focus their operations on what is really required of them by the customer!

8 **Changed outlook:** Marketing can become the central business function, which increases the firm's competitiveness.

All activity should be focused on the impact on the customer.

9 **Staffing changes:** Staff need to change to adopt the new philosophy. Becoming successfully customer-focused requires the involvement and commitment of all your people.

You ignore marketing at your peril. You cannot assume that you are doing 'good' marketing just because you are still in business. You could simply be selling lots because you are giving your product away! You could be missing profitable opportunities right now, simply because you are spending too much time on everything but your customer!

Case study

Jim Hibbert's TKD, a Chicago-based web design company, grew to fifteen employees and a turnover of $2 million in eleven months. All sales had come from word-of-mouth referral. But suddenly the future looked grim. The team that had got the business so far did not have the skills required for the next stage of growth, there were serious working capital problems, and there had been no proactive marketing to date.

Jim had no idea where the next sales were going to come from, as he had never had to go looking for sales, and was nervous about the capability of his team, and suddenly things were slowing down. Jim went off and put together the firm's first marketing plan. For the first time he analysed where most of the profits were coming from and which work was the most profitable. By looking at the business through the customer's eyes he was able to design a communication and branding programme focusing on the needs of a specific industry. He was also able to make some pretty serious decisions about his future team.

Jim reflects: 'I should have known better than to be so reactive – we nearly lost everything but now we are stronger than ever. The imaginary customer is now the start and the finish of everything that we do. The customer informs us as to what we should do next – we have regained control of the business and we run the business rather than the business running us.'

Case study

Two years ago, Altruistic employed nine people with a turnover of $950,000. Today the company employs 68 people and has a turnover in excess of £4 million. Altruistic's success is due, in part, to help from a business adviser.

Altruistic is a leading supplier of campaign management software and business services. The company is particularly strong in the financial-services sector, where its key product, DirectHit, is extensively used to produce the best possible results from customer direct marketing. The market is growing rapidly as more companies see the sales potential of targeted mailings based on sophisticated database management.

After three years of impressive growth, Altruistic encountered a pitfall that is familiar to many young companies – a focus on tactical matters at the expense of a long-term strategy. They needed to transform their approach.

The business adviser recommended a customer perception survey, which he personally carried out among key customers, using a specially designed questionnaire. The survey provided valuable feedback on pricing and positioning.

As the managing director Pete Barker explains, 'We found out that our understanding of the marketplace is what earns us higher ratings than the competition. This is our unique selling point [USP]. Customers may say that they want a software system but they are actually looking for the answer to a business question. These results indicated that we should concentrate more on communicating our USP and also that we could afford to raise our prices. We have done both, very successfully.'

The lesson from these two case studies is that often we are so busy running our businesses that we forget to step back and look at what we should really be doing. We spend too much time 'delivering', thinking about the doing, the operations, and sometimes forget to look at what the customers want from us. Spend more time seeing the business through the eyes of the customer.

Marketing strategy – some crunch marketing questions

In the long run, marketing is the only logical and sustainable option. To ignore your customer seems foolhardy.

The concept of marketing, satisfying customer needs, can be broken down into four parts.

1 What is the need that must be satisfied?

- [ ] Who has the need? Find out all you can about the profile of your customers. For example, group them by age, sex, job position, income, geography, reading habits or other common trait.

- [ ] Why do they need it? If you understand what they need the product/service for, then you can design the product to help them even more. For example, businesspeople use laptop computers for working while travelling, so everything about the design should encourage ease of use when travelling.

- [ ] When/why/who buys? A knowledge of when and why the purchase takes place will help you to help the customer to buy from you. Many decisions are seasonal as a consequence of other events. For instance, printers are often bought with computers; a new radio device for listening to rugby referees' radio communication with officials will be sold just before matches.

- [ ] What will influence the need? The more you understand the pressures or levers on the purchaser, the more you can affect the buying process. Social, political and many other influences affect the need. For instance, drink-drive legislation will affect the demand for, say, taxis or personal breathalysers.

- [ ] How will demand change? Being able to predict future needs helps you to develop the relationship with the customer. For example, a hi-fi manufacturer can keep clients aware of new technology products; a refuse truck manufacturer can fit safety features that comply with forthcoming legislation.

2 What are the products or services that will satisfy demand?

- [ ] What particular aspects of the product/service are important? For instance, many householders are more interested in what a music system *looks* like than what it *sounds* like.

What is it that customers are buying? For example, people don't buy a Rolex watch simply to tell the time – they are a fashion accessory.

What are the product features? It is important to understand the characteristics of the product. For example, a skateboard might be made from a heat-sealed, bonded plywood.

What are the product benefits? Benefits are why the customer buys the product, what the product does for the user. For instance, special plywood makes a skateboard stronger and more flexible, which means that it lasts longer and yet is still very flexible.

At what price? How much is the customer willing to pay? What will the customer pay for such a product? Because of the value associated with a brand name such as Gucci, customers are willing to pay a premium price; conversely, commodity products with little brand value command low prices, such as refuse bags. This is why so many people brand everything from milk to eggs to T-shirts.

3 Who/what is the competition?

Who are they? The more you know about your competitors, the less of a surprise you will get. For instance, are they competing directly with you, or are they even aware of your existence?

How are they performing financially? This information helps you to assess your next moves. For example, an underperforming competitor may be thinking of getting out of your market, may have staff who are about to be made redundant, or may consider being bought out.

How does your product/service compare? To be more precise, how does your product compare in terms of features, build and of course in benefits to the customer? Flights of Fancy, for instance, know that they lead their market in terms of offering new, innovative and witty gift products – they need to maintain this edge to stay ahead of the competition.

How are competitors perceived by your customers? If you can find out what your customers think of the competition then you can adapt your offering accordingly. For instance, customer satisfaction surveys can identify what customers like and dislike about your competition.

How do they perceive you? Do competitors fear you or are they even aware of your presence? Commission a student to undertake a so-called market/industry survey – they can interview key players (i.e. your competitors) and find out who is seen as market leader and how they view your business!

4 How are the need and the product best connected?

How is your identity branded/perceived? What do customers think of your product offering and what it represents? Focusing on the needs of companies who have found computer training dull, Happy Computers is known as a leading provider of fun but effective computer training.

How are the product/services branded? The most important issue about branding is how your target customer sees your brand. Famous errors include the fact that 'Coca-Cola' in China means either 'bite the wax tadpole' or 'female horse stuffed with wax'; Wang Computers' customer care system was called 'Wang Care'; Colgate's 'Cue' in France was the name of a porno magazine.

How is it packaged? Packaging is often as important as the product itself. For instance, luxury items have luxury wrappings to reflect the supposedly premium product.

How is it promoted? Your choice of promotion channels will determine who sees the product and how they see it, so select your channels carefully. Bridget Janes Inc., the CV-writing service, advertises only in the better, business newspapers and hence adverts are seen only by its desired customers, middle and senior managers looking at a career change.

How is it sold? How is it available? Different routes to market apply to the different customer segments. Macromedia, for example, offer fully working software with a one month's free trial – the intention is that the user will have had such a good experience that they will want to own and use the software for themselves. The software is available on the net and on a free CD when attached to various business and Internet magazines.

Marketing strategy?

Like any other strategy, your strategy for marketing is your route map for getting there. The fundamental question, then, is to write down your marketing vision. In other words:

Why which customers will choose us?

Write down:

1. Your market position now, and in the future
2. Your customer position now and in the future
3. How you will achieve and sustain this new position

In any business you are trying to create a product offering, or more specifically a brand. A brand is defined as:

- Signs by which you are known and remembered
- A bundle of explicit/implicit promises
- A reflection of personality
- A statement of position

Brand is important because you cannot *not* communicate. Everything you say or do tells other people something about your business. The brand has a life beyond that of the owner. A good brand will increase the effectiveness of communication; it will improve and help awareness.

Ask these questions:

1. Is the business/brand distinct? Is it continuing to demonstrate its difference?
2. Is the business/brand proposition meaningful and right for the target audience?
3. How highly do customers think of and feel about the business? What is their perception of its quality and of its 'momentum' – its growth in popularity?
4. How many people know the business/brand and, more important, truly understand what it is about?

If you wish to create this brand you need to ask some further questions. Establish, in relation to customer needs and any competitive offerings (brands), what is the positioning that you have or, rather, would like to have in the customer's mind. A good starting point is to define:

1 To whom does the brand appeal? Who is it that you are aiming the brand at? Your communications should be 'talking to' these people in a way that they understand and can relate to. For example, a health insurance company that focuses on selling to retired people will 'communicate' in a way that is accessible to the particular age group: TV adverts will use recognisable personalities and make reference to issues that are meaningful to the age group.

2 What does the brand offer? If your brand offers the same as all the others, then why should people bother to come to your business? You need to separate yourself from the rest. In an age of email communication, Gerry Bentley prides himself on individual attention to all clients – all envelopes are handwritten, in fountain pen, to emphasise individual attention.

3 Why is it better than other offerings? You want to be seen as better, cheaper, quicker or faster than the rest – you want to be in the customer's mind when they are thinking of buying from your market. Try to position yourself as the 'first' in the region, or the 'newest', or the 'fastest'. Be clear to your client about the benefit that you are offering them. For example, 'Freshly made pizza to your door in thirty minutes or your money back' is a great slogan. It tells the customer exactly what they are going to get and challenges the perennial customer problem of getting sad, tired pizza an hour after it's ordered.

If you can answer these questions, and it is no mean task to address them, then you are a long way towards being able to define your marketing vision and hence your strategy to achieve it.

Case study

Robert Haberman's Robert's Fudge Factory was founded in 1983. The company manufactures fudge. As annual turnover passed the £1 million mark, he started to see sales even out. The company took a series of knocks, which culminated in what Robert described as 'the seven-month summer' – nobody bought fudge because of a phenomenally hot summer.

To secure his business, Robert knew that he had to grow. As important, he recognised that it had to mature and change. Having asked the questions above, he identified three main areas of change:

- The way the product was presented
- New product development
- Widening the customer base

The business's traditional customer base, small single shops, was too narrowing and limiting. Targeting larger outlets such as the chains seemed to be the answer.

'Making the change from selling into mom-and-pop stores to bigger ones was part of the plan I developed,' explains Haberman. No one else was selling fudge to these people! That in turn meant looking at new product development, and new packaging 'and for that I needed an injection of cash'. Enter a friendly local bank that was willing to lend the necessary money.

The focus on selling to the bigger players forced changes on the sales operation, effectively transforming it. The ratio between sales by distributors to van sales turned upside down.

Other changes followed. Labels were outdated; a new range (tested at a major trade fair) was immediately launched. As well as looking to new markets, Robert has been carefully cultivating old ones.

'Developing your existing client base is more cost-effective than going out and getting new clients. You need to look after what you have as well as develop new clients. The hard work and the risk have paid dividends.'

Haberman had to ask himself a lot of tough questions to figure out what he had to do to the business. There is no rule book but the process of asking the questions challenges you to do things in a different or better way. To say that the process is smooth and easy would be dishonest, but if you search enough, you will find ways to satisfy your customers in a way that is better than the way that your competition are doing it!

The Ansoff Matrix

I started my career as a sound recording engineer. The job became easy for me to understand when I was told that there were only two things you can do with sound in a recording studio: make it go up and down and make it go on and off.

In business there are only three new things you can do to grow a business:

1 Change the product or service you deliver (new product development: same market, new product).
2 Change the markets you sell to (market extension: new markets, same product).
3 Combine the two (diversification: new market, new product).

Number Four would be 'Do what you are already doing but better, faster or cheaper (market penetration: same market, same product) – but that is not a new direction.

There's a tried and tested model used by many to analyse and develop market and product strategies for growing businesses developed by the management teacher Igor Ansoff.

As depicted in the table opposite, the Ansoff Matrix offers a logical framework to plot different strategies for growth.

Ansoff, a famous strategist, plotted two directions (market and service/product) on to axes and created a matrix framework to assess different strategies. In broad terms the four key strategic choices were:

1 New product development
2 Market extension
3 Diversification
4 Market penetration.

Ansoff Matrix

markets: services/ products:	existing	extension	new
existing	4		2
modification			
new	1		3

The Ansoff Matrix shows you possible opportunities that your business can pursue. The Matrix reveals that there are levels of risk attached to any new direction.

There are levels of greater and greater risk that can be drawn as you move away from the top left-hand corner of the Matrix. As with isobars on a weather map, the risk increases as you move away from the 'comfort zone'. The Matrix shows that the levels of risk increase as you move towards the bottom right-hand corner. So make sure that you have really thought through the consequences of your potentially higher-risk strategy.

Although the bottom right-hand corner of the Matrix often looks the most exciting and potentially profitable, it is also the most risky.

In the majority of cases, the most successful strategy is relatively uncomplicated. The highest-risk strategy is diversification (new market, new product). Alarm bells ring when companies seek to combine the twin risks of entering new markets with new products. While this option seems very attractive, it may simply be an illusion.

In the cold light of day, companies who pursue the sexy (new product, new market), bottom right-hand corner diversification option are often ignoring the less sexy but safer top left-hand corner option of continuing to sell their existing product in their existing marketplace.

Checklist – to find niches and opportunities

- [ ] Neglected markets where, say, customer needs have outpaced provision, e.g. hand-built cars such as Morgan, importing organic wines.

- [ ] Unfilled need, e.g. work away from the office creates a demand for laptop computers, the creation of Pokémon card swapshops.

- [ ] Disadvantages in existing products, e.g. caffeine in coffee leads to decaffeinated coffee, short life of cut flowers leads to demand for sachets containing long-life crystals for flower water.

- [ ] Omission in otherwise well-served markets, e.g. paper napkins, outdoor workers require robust mobile phones.

- [ ] Extensions or new formats for proven lines, e.g. T-shirts, scarves and sweatshirts for rugby supporters' club, Weight Watcher soups/Heinz.

- [ ] Technological breakthroughs, e.g. email-driven mentoring and business support, special covers for reducing mobile-phone radiation, bagless vacuum cleaners.

- [ ] Transferable success from other markets, e.g. yo-yo from Hawaii, Tapas bar from Spain.

- [ ] More economical ways of satisfying wants now being met expensively, e.g. temporary office accommodation, freelance IT managers that you buy in for a day or so a month.

- [ ] Less economical ways of satisfying wants that are being met only adequately: Ben & Jerry's ice cream, designer-tailored football boots.

- [ ] Copy substitutes: copy the competitive offerings, e.g. Wild Oats copied theme pubs and made board games and newspapers available in the restaurant, local delicatessen starts sandwich round to maintain sales.

- [ ] Do the opposite of traditional industry norms to emphasis the difference: Gerry Bentley adopted a 'pen-and-ink' approach to all communications in the face of database-driven and computer communications that his competition were using; the chef Andreas Honore serves all meals to the tables of his restaurant guests.

- [ ] Change the product appeal and/or reinventing yourself, e.g. Lucozade changes itself from being a sick person's drink to being a healthy person's fitness drink, Viewfrom moves from satisfying the mass market to appealing to professional athletes.

☐ Change the use of the product, e.g. isopropyl alcohol branded as video tape head cleaner and sold at ten times higher price; bicarbonate of soda packaged and branded as refrigerator cleaner.

☐ Add complementary products or services, e.g. CD shops selling books and merchandise to complement CDs available, dentist selling general and specialist toothbrushes.

Case study

NJ Filters (NY), manufacturer of air-conditioning filters, turned over $11 million a year. The managing director saw an opportunity, in a business advertising magazine, to manufacture and install specialist waste filter systems to landfill sites in the Middle East. This was far from core business; indeed it was a case of new product, new market. This strategy sustained heavy losses, as the firm was not able to accommodate the new demands made on it by the entry into new products/services.

Case study

A California-based retail computer company that specialised in selling PCs to the home market attempted to sell very expensive mainframe computers to large corporate organisations. This was a strategy that sent the company straight to the bottom right-hand corner of the Ansoff Matrix. Within three months it was in the insolvency courts. It simply did not realise how different the new offering was from the old one. Because they were both computers the company (incorrectly) assumed that the same skills would be required to sell them, but the types of buyers and their needs were totally different, as was the product and its features.

In both instances, the diversifications sustained severe losses – the companies were simply not prepared for the demands of the new situation.

Case study

MisterWeb spent three years developing and nurturing a website design business and had grown to employ 23 coders and account managers. The owner-manager, Phil, had always had a potential business partnership in mind for a start-up web-based business for the air-conditioning industry (of which he had no experience). Spending roughly half-a-day a week on the new project, Phil finally realised several things:

> ■ The start-up is really bottom right-hand corner of the Ansoff Matrix and therefore high-risk.
>
> ■ Given limited resources, Phil was not prepared to risk the existing business for the new one.
>
> ■ There was more than enough money to be made by systematically sticking to the top left-hand corner of the matrix.

Phil wanted to get involved with the start-up but he decided that he was not prepared to risk the existing business by chasing a whim. It was time to grow up and make sensible decisions.

ACTION POINT

1 Looking at your business's growth to date, plot your business growth according to the Ansoff Matrix. Has it been by product development or by market development, or by focusing in that bottom right-hand box? Have there been lots of little incremental steps on the way or big quantum leaps? How have you coped with and managed this type of change?

2 Looking at you business plans and options for the future, do they continue the trend to date? What is the consequence for managing the growth? How are you going to grow the business and what is the associated risk? If there are a series of choices to be made, then you can compare the different options using the Matrix.

Marketing strategy is about trade-offs and choice – the Ansoff Matrix may help you to make those tough decisions.

Checklist – marketing meets business strategy

Decide what you want to do with the business:

☐ Make it grow?
☐ Keep it stable?
☐ Decrease its size?

How are you going to be different from the rest?

☐ By cost leadership (by being the cheapest with the lowest costs)?
☐ By being uniquely different (by finding your niche)?
☐ By concentration and focus (on a few key products or services)?

Frequently asked questions

Q. We already do advertising, so we don't need this stuff, do we?

A. Marketing is not just advertising. Marketing is about finding out exactly whom you are trying to sell to, and why and how they would like to buy from you. And getting them to do it. 'Identifying and understanding and satisfying customer needs (profitably)' is the definition. The more you look at marketing, the better you will be able to focus your efforts effectively on getting the sort of results that you are trying to achieve.

Q. You make marketing sound like yet another cost. Exactly when am I supposed to run my business? By the time I've spent money on consultants and graphics designers, there won't be any money left over as profit.

A. Much marketing can be done in house, using existing people and information. As you try to understand your business through the customers' eyes so you are able to fine-tune your offering and so increase the chances of a sale.

Q. I brought a marketing consultant into my business once and he was useless. I am not trying that lark again. Are marketing consultants really necessary?

A. Once bitten, twice shy, eh? Well don't assume that all of marketing is a waste of time because you had a bad experience with a rogue consultant. The more time that you put into thinking about your marketing, the better the results. Often an expert will save you time and money and save you the effort of reinventing the wheel.

Q. I don't need marketing: I need sales. When we've sorted the sales out then we can ponce around with this marketing stuff. Isn't sales effort more important than marketing effort?

A. Sales effort is often a waste of time if it is not focused and targeted correctly. Marketing is the design and preparation work that should be put in place so that your sales effort can be more successful.

Q. This Ansoff business is all a bit esoteric – how can it help my business? How would I use this in my business?

A. This Matrix enables you to compare, contrast and discuss different options. At the end of the day, it is you who decide when something is 'new' rather than a 'modification', but the point is that the framework gets the old grey cells thinking about the options for the business in a relatively structured manner. Be clear about the different levels of risk attached to different options

Q. I've got business opportunities in virtually every box. What does that mean?

A. Remember that what was 'new' business last year becomes 'existing' business today. It is possible to be working in all the boxes – everything seems to interrelate and if it's well managed then it is possible to work in that manner. However, it is normally easier to have a focused strategy working in a maximum of two boxes – otherwise you end up spreading your resources too thinly! Remember that truly effective strategy tends to be very simple – getting real benefits by exploiting one's niche and corner of expertise. The more you try to stretch your brand, the harder it is to satisfy all the various stakeholders – unless of course you have an exceptional brand, but even then your brand will not be infinitely elastic!

Summary

Businesses must never lose sight of who their customers are and what their customers want from them! If you ask the right questions, you get answers and you can use these answers to develop your business effectively.

Get the whole business focusing on customers and their needs.

The Ansoff Matrix is a tool for assessing risk – the bottom right-hand corner of the Matrix (diversifying) implies greater risk – it is leaving the 'comfort zone', which is never the easiest of things to do. Because the Matrix is such a visual tool, it enables managers to talk about and understand how future (and past) strategies for growth will have different 'risks' attached to them. It aids the business to make the appropriate decisions while better understanding the implications.

CHAPTER SEVEN

Bright marketing

Bright marketing focuses on branding. Bright marketing is not all about big budgets – it is all about big impact. This chapter helps you to think through your approach to your customers.

The bright-marketing framework is a tool for looking at what you are trying to communicate, and to whom. It is not rocket science. By answering the questions you will realise what you need to do in order to fine-tune and improve your marketing activities. Any improvements will be seen in increased profitability.

Starting with brands and branding, you are able to tighten and improve your brand proposition, which improves the effectiveness of subsequent sales efforts.

Branding is all about creating a distinct personality for your business and telling the world about it. Brands matter. They have a life beyond the owner and they increase awareness as well as communication.

- Branding is . . . the signs by which you are known and remembered.
- Branding is . . . a reflection of personality.
- Branding is . . . a statement of position.

Everything you do says something about you. You cannot *not* communicate – the messages leak out like radioactivity – so you must try to decide what messages you want to be seen. The market is hopelessly crowded nowadays, so, as a result, branding is more important than it ever was.

Bright-marketing questions

The following bright-marketing questions look at why and how you approach your customers. Some of the questions may look simplistic but spending time exploring the answers will help you to define what it is that you are trying to do. Apply the questions on their own or in the context of the 100-day plan. (See Part Two, Session Fourteen.)

1 What does your brand say?

You need to test out what your existing brand says to the observer. While you think you know what you were trying to say when designing your own logo, website, packaging or headed notepaper, the key test is what other people see when they look at your materials.

ACTION POINT

The one-minute brand test

You can get someone else to do this to your own 'branded materials' (headed notepaper, advertisement) or do it to someone else's materials.

Take the materials and spend one minute looking at them. Write down anything that springs to mind about them:

☐ What does it remind you of? Banks? Skateboarding? Fun? Cricket?

☐ What does it 'say' to you? Old-fashioned? Trendy? Retro? Sexy? Dull?

☐ Whom does it appeal to? Men? Children? Workaholics? Phone users?

☐ What does it say about the company? Modern? Grey? Reliable? Design-led?

The one-minute brand test is valid in as much as the tester's opinions are by definition his/her opinions. You can run the same test with a larger audience to get a feel for how well the materials work (though the customer's eyes).

2 What is the benefit to the customers/consumers?

When we make a product or offer a service, we are often more concerned with the features that make it special. (By 'feature', I mean a technological twist, or a unique function, or a special way of doing the job.) Customers, however, tend to be more interested in benefits. A benefit explains what the product does for the customer. To translate a feature into a benefit you have to take the feature and then explain what it means to the customer:

Feature	Benefit
Toughened surface	It won't get damaged
UH-treated	It will stay fresher for longer
Twelve-hour battery time	You will not need to keep recharging it

Customers buy benefits, not features. Unsuccessful sellers tend to focus too much on the features of a product rather than concentrate on customer benefits. This is a common mistake of businesses, losing sight of why they are *in* business, and who actually pays the bills at the end of the day!

ACTION POINT

What are the benefits of the features that you have in your product or service? Write down a list, features in one column and, for the other column, work out what are the benefits of each feature.

This exercise ensures that you are focusing on the product/service through the customer's eyes. Keep asking what the feature *means to the customer*. Ask the question, 'So what?' to try to help this process along. Let's do it.

Feature: fast. What does this mean to the customer? What's the benefit? It's quicker than the competition. So what? Well, it's an opportunity to be seen as better than the competition. So what? It means that there is a chance to sell more. So what? Well, it means more profits.

3 What business are you in?

A training colleague thought that he was in the business of transmitting ideas. He was wrong. People attended his seminars to improve their businesses. Once you understand what business you are really in, then you can be more effective in delivering the product or service.

For instance, bar owners believe they are in the business of selling drinks. Wrong! The successful bar owners have reorganised their businesses to cater for the needs of particular age groups. They are really in the entertainment business. Alcohol brands for the young say much about the sort of person the drinkers think they are. Similarly, universities should be offering a whole-person education and career path; a software package should help you run a better office.

Understanding what business you are really in makes it so much easier to focus your efforts.

The question 'What business are you really in?' asks you to think through why people come to you and what they expect to get from you. Think about the whole package that you are selling (confidence, affiliation needs, reliability, after-sales service, brand, price, value for money), and not just the product itself.

4 Who is the product for?

Until you can define whom the product is for, you cannot determine whether you have got the branding right. This question is not always straightforward. For instance, often the purchaser is not the same as the user, and the person who makes the purchasing decision is not the same as the purchaser. So, training is often selected by the training office, the customer. It is consumed by the workers, the consumers. It is paid for by the finance director.

The question that needs to be addressed is, for whom should you be designing your communications? Or should you address the different audiences with different messages?

Make sure that you are clear about whom you are targeting your communications material at. Make sure that you are satisfying their needs and talking to them in a language that they understand. Demonstrate the benefits that they would be interested in. Is there some way that you could be doing this better than the way that you are doing it now?

5 What is your position?

How do you differ from your competitors? As a consequence of understanding how you differ, you can then focus your communications on what makes you different. Remember that if you are the same as your competition, then why should clients bother to buy from you?

Establishing the business's position is a three-part process.

5.a List your competitors and list which customers or customer segments each competitor is aimed at

Draw up a list of your key competitors. Next to each competitor, list the customers or target customer segments that the competitor focuses on. What will emerge is that different competitors are focusing on different niches or subsectors of the market.

5.b Write down your niche

In other words, which customers or customer segment are you aimed at? Be specific about who you aim your business activities at. Consider your key competitors for those customers. Often we work so hard to get the product out of the factory gate that we forget to remind ourselves exactly what we are trying to do. More importantly we need to have a thorough understanding of the competitive environment that we are competing in.

5.c Establish your position

Establishing your position is a very ambiguous process, which helps you to understand your competitive environment. The position is mapped out in a brand positioning matrix. The box has two different axes that allow you to map out the competing businesses according to how they score on the axes. At its simplest level, you decide the titles of the axes. The purpose is to find axes that emphasise the difference between you and your competitors (in the eyes of the customer).

What do you put on the axes? It is time for a bit of creativity. You need to look at your business through your customers' eyes. If you interviewed a customer, what might be the sort of criteria that they would use to measure you, compared with others in your industry? Smarter? Faster? Higher-tech? More rigorous? Cheaper? Cleaner? Friendlier?

Take several of the criteria that might be applied to your business and see which ones create some kind of a space between you and the competition. For instance, if the criterion is fast, does this suggest that most of your competitors are much slower? If the criterion is younger, does this suggest that your competition is mostly much older?

Eventually you will have two criteria for the two axes. You might have: bespoke–standard solution; local–national; traditional–hyper-modern, hi-tech–low-tech; metropolitan–provincial; indoors–outdoors; cheap–expensive; people-led–market-led, and so on. You need to go through the motions of doing this exercise on paper. Reading about it will not make you get a better understanding of your business. Finding the right combination of axes is the tough part. If you are able to separate yourself 'from the rest', then this becomes the difference that you can focus on.

The case study below will explain how the matrix works in action.

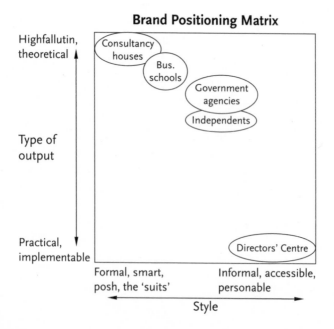

Brand Positioning Matrix

Case study

The Directors' Centre is a new management consultancy trying to establish some kind of 'uniqueness'. All consultancies, small or large, claim to offer unique, bespoke solutions tailored to the client's needs, working in partnership with the client. In fact it is almost impossible to differentiate the competition because everyone makes the same promises. So, the task was to find a way to separate the business from the similar-sounding competitors.

After several hours of trying out different combinations of headings for the axes, the company's senior management team finally found a set of headings that would separate themselves out from the rest. The headings chosen were:

> ■ Type of output/work done
> ■ Style of dealing with clients

Competitors

Big consultancy houses, e.g. KPMG, Andersen
Business schools
Government agencies
Independent freelance consultants

Axis 1: type of output

A scale between very theoretical and very practical hands-on:

Consultancy houses:	very theoretical
Business schools:	fairly theoretical
Government agencies:	midway between the two
Independents:	slightly less theoretical
The Directors' Centre:	very hands-on, practical

Axis 2: style

A scale between very formal, the 'suits' and very informal:

Consultancy houses:	the designer suits
Business schools:	the jackets and ties
Government agencies:	midway between the two
Independents:	midway between the two
The Directors' Centre:	very informally dressed

If you plot the two axes on to a matrix and plot the various positions of the differing competitors your map looks as above. What you can see from the positioning matrix is that your selection of axes has enabled you to define a unique positioning. This can be used to emphasise the difference between the business and its competitors.

For instance, your advertising copy or sales pitch could run along the lines of: 'Whereas most consultants are the theoretical "suits", we are quite the opposite. We are very informal and focus on practical outcomes.' Or, 'If you want a theory-oriented consultant, go to the others. But if you want a consultant who is more interested in practical, hands-on results, then come to us!'

The positioning exercise enables you to define your own niche. And the purpose of developing your niche is to make your business different, or even unique, in its category.

6. What is your brand positioning statement?

Having attempted the positioning exercise, you can use the results to create or develop your brand positioning statement (BPS), a simple one-page summary of the key elements that make up your brand personality and your brand proposition. This 'worksheet' helps your thinking about what attributes your brand should be carrying. The thinking about the issues is probably more important than the final output. The process considers establishing what you are and what you are not. It helps to define what you want your brand to represent.

Your brand positioning statement should consider the following:

- [ ] Market description: describes the marketplace that the brand is meant to be living in. It is the market description that customers would use, e.g. retail sports goods, construction materials.
- [ ] Target audience: pinpoints the people you are trying to get to look at your brand, the people you are selling to, e.g. sports players, builders' merchants.
- [ ] Brand discriminators: describes what benefits the brand is best at delivering, e.g. honest advice, reliable delivery.

☐ Core customer proposition: refers to the emotional and functional aspects of what is being offered to the customer, e.g. security, confidence.

☐ Brand differentiators: considers how the brand is different, e.g. all staff qualified, unique guarantees.

☐ Brand personality: is about the image and associations that it should create, e.g. fit and sporty, reliable and trustworthy.

Case study

Below is the brand positioning statement as created for the Directors' Centre:

Brand positioning statement (BPS)

Market description:	Consultancy
Target audience:	Blue-chip businesses; senior managers
Brand discriminators:	Honest, practical
Core customer proposition:	Practical, straightforward, not high-theory
Brand differentiator:	Focus on entrepreneurship
Brand personality:	Challenging, open, ethical

7. A guerrilla marketing audit?

The final part of the bright-marketing jigsaw is to do a guerrilla marketing audit. The word 'guerrilla' is used to imply an 'underground', unconventional, simple yet effective approach to beating your competitors to get to customers.

Having done the earlier sections of this chapter, you should now have no difficulty in answering these fundamental questions.

1 Who is your target customer?
2 What problem are you solving for them?
3 What benefits are you offering that your competitors are not offering?
4 Why should customers spend money with you rather than with your competitors?
5 Two sentences that describe what your business stands for are . . .?

All of this work will get you to feel more comfortable about answering those key questions about the competitive advantage that you must develop:

- ☐ Will your target audience perceive what you believe to be a competitive advantage as a competitive advantage?
- ☐ Do you offer something different from what your competitors offer?
- ☐ Will people honestly benefit from this advantage?
- ☐ Will they believe your statements about this advantage?
- ☐ Will this advantage motivate people to buy from you?

Adding value to the brand

The most effective brands are associated with feelings – look at the Marlboro Experience, or the Starbucks Experience, or the Levi's Experience. A smaller business is able to offer more 'experience' than the big businesses: you have more contact with the clients and suppliers and your business is run by real people rather than anonymous employees. This is one of the great things about small businesses.

To add value to your brand, try to sell Memorable Sensory Experiences (MSEs). If possible, make the business transaction into something enjoyable and memorable.

For example, Transworld Skate Shop in Denver talked my son through every part of the bespoke skateboard that they were building for him and then they let us watch it being built. Ailsa Handmade Chocolates took me downstairs to watch their chocolates actually being made. I am their number-one fan! Happy Computers give their delegates, who are learning to use computers, ice creams at the coffee and tea breaks.

Case study

Andrew Waterfall runs Improvision Ltd, employing 35 people, making and selling modular software for scientific imaging for the biomedical research departments of universities. Based in the Midlands, the whole business was set up with the intention of providing the best solution in the world.

Andrew quietly set about designing a product that would actually be the best in class. Three years later the product had made the business a tidy income in Europe but Andrew wanted more. He looked to America for the next stage of growth. Everyone told him that his little 25-man business would get eaten alive in the States. The business had grown organically to date and America looked like a potential hole in the ground to throw money into. Andrew approached the whole situation rationally and logically.

'The whole episode was an exercise in planning and preparation. We knew that we had to minimise the downside so made a couple of key decisions. We based the American operation in Boston – opportunity abounded everywhere in the States but we decided to focus exclusively on building up our reputation from a core centre. We knew the market inside out and we knew how and why our product outclassed the competition.

'Even against the big boys, our product is better able to give the customer what they want. Our customer service and attention to detail far outstrips the competition and our product actually does what is required of it – in an easier, friendlier, and more productive way than the competition.

'I always knew that we were going to create the number-one product in the world. Everything was leading up to the assault on America, and it has paid off!'

A classic example of having a Big Hairy Audacious Goal – a BHAG! 'We take pride in the development of easy-to-use, quality solutions with eye-popping innovation. The lesson is that you need to have grit, determination and a really clear, ambitious vision to stretch and challenge you.'

Andrew's tenacity and hard work were rewarded with a sales increase of staggering proportions and an award for outstanding commercial achievement, the Queen's Award for Enterprise.

Communicating your business to others – the elevator statement

Piecing together your elevator statement is a great way to start thinking about what you are trying to do with the business.

An elevator statement is a succinct explanation of what you and your business do. How well can you explain what you do to a stranger? Do you convince the stranger about your business or do you open your mouth and splutter forth a whole series of indecipherable jargon and gobbledegook that leaves the listener none the wiser?

Your elevator statement should be easily understandable. If you are in doubt about its simplicity, try the 'thirteen-year-old' test. Your statement should be easily understood by my thirteen-year-old son.

Case study

Mr Chow's: 'We run the only chain of city-centre cafés that offer a choice of delicious, freshly cooked $10 main meals from the countries of Thailand, Malaysia, China and Japan – our customers are young businesspeople working in the city centre who find oriental food exciting.'

Case study

The Lighting Company: 'We are the number-one company for the sale, hire and repair of every type of and size of lighting that might be required in a movie.'

Action point

Write down your elevator statement.

Instructions

You bump into a stranger as you get into an elevator at the airport. The stranger asks, 'What does your company do?' You have 30 seconds to answer the question. Write your answer below. My elevator statement is: 'My company . . .'

which means . . .

Checklist – elevator statement

Does your elevator statement:

- [ ] Sound convincing?
- [ ] Explain what your business does?

- [ ] Roll off the tongue smoothly?
- [ ] Make the listener understand what your business does?
- [ ] Pass the 'thirteen-year-old' understanding test?

Checklist – bright marketing

- [ ] Differentiate your product – the famous Unique Selling Proposition, or USP. Why should customers buy from you and not from somebody else? The difference can lie in the goods or services (yo-yos with clutches are a perfect example) or in, say, delivery (American surfwear from California by mail order in Europe). But without the USP you'll be a mere, much less promising 'me too'.

- [ ] Identify your market segment. There's no better example than DollarBrand focusing on 16–20-year-old aspiring surfers in Europe. Try to keep looking for something else you can supply to your devoted audience.

- [ ] Promote with purpose. Promotion and branding must tell people why they desire the offering and how they can buy – and must deliver that message incessantly and consistently.

Frequently asked questions

Q. I know that my logo and stuff may not be great, but once people know me then I usually get the business. You haven't mentioned logos and design directly, so what are you trying to say?

A. My point is simply that you cannot help sending out messages to your potential customers by the way that you choose to present your business. So, you need to be aware of how your business is being seen through the eyes of the potential customer. Your presentation does say a lot about how you choose to present yourself; implicitly it sends people messages about how you do business. Just be aware that your choice of logo sends out a certain set of messages and make sure that the messages that are received are the ones that you intend to communicate.

Q. Branding is for the big boys, not for little businesses. How do you expect me to brand my retail outlet?

A. Wrong. Branding is not just for the big boys. In a world where all products are looking increasingly similar, it is the process of branding that enables you to look different and to focus on specific target audiences – this is the route to success.

Q. Branding clearly isn't effective. Isn't that why the Big Boys spend so much money on it?

A. Wrong again. Branding clearly does work and that is why they spend so much money on it. Strong, effective branding usually means that you are able to charge premium prices or do more business.

Q. Is your so-called bright marketing about getting a new logo and paying for the privilege of new stationery etc.?

A. No, all we are trying to do is make sure that you are getting the 'biggest bang for your buck'. Most businesses do not reflect on whether their communication methods are up to speed. It is so easy to waste resources on what we think is a good image. So, check out whether you are sending out the right messages. In fact, make sure that you know why customers should come to you and make sure you know why you are better than your competitors. After all, if you aren't offering benefits that your competition aren't offering then why should people bother to spend money with you?

Summary

Bright marketing is all about thinking through your approach to your customers. This can be done on your own or in a workshop setting. The cost of quality thinking is very low. The cost of not improving the quality of your thinking may be very high in the long run!

CHAPTER EIGHT

Focus your people on customers

Turning theory into reality is a real issue in marketing. A major part of success in marketing is getting your people to buy into the importance of focusing on the needs of your customers.

All the up-tempo marketing hype certainly seems to have hit the mark. We all know what the reply is when we cry out the challenge, 'What is it that every so-called modern company wants right now?' 'What we want,' comes back the reply, 'are customers and employees who are loyal and excited by what we do. What we want to see is commitment and a pride that shines through in everything we do. We want the phone lines jammed and the corridors awash with customers desperately wanting to do business with *us*!'

The reality is somewhat different. Most businesses have a few employees who do love their work and their customers and take real pride in their work – but, to be honest, just how many? Twenty per cent of them, or ten, or fewer? Most employees still leave their brains in the staff car parks when they come to work. Pretty sad really.

Craven's '20:60:20 Rule of Staff Development' kicks in with a vengeance – generally, the top 20 per cent will be with you; 60 per cent will follow the top 20 per cent (eventually); and 20 per cent will never want to be moved. It's one thing having a few of the fine people, the water-walkers, in your organisation, but how do you get to have more of them? Can you make more of your people care? Or do you have to employ new people?

The answer to these questions is pretty much stating the obvious. If you want your people to care about your customers then you have to set in motion a programme that proves that you care about your people.

Create a place where your staff feel valued and encouraged and then they will pass on their enthusiasm for the business to your customers.

Why customers quit – why we can't keep them

We know why most customers quit. Three per cent move away, geographically; 5 per cent develop relationships with other suppliers; 9 per cent leave for competitive reasons; and only 14 per cent are dissatisfied with the product or service. And yet a staggering 69 per cent (yes, 69 per cent!) quit because of an attitude of indifference towards them! They believe we don't care.

Meanwhile the average company has to spend six times as much to attract one new sale than to get a sale from an existing client.

What can you do?

You must design a programme (possibly involving someone from the outside) so that your customers get an experience (from your staff) that makes them believe that you do care about them.

Step One: Create a workplace where all this naturally happens – where your people (internal customers) are treated as well as you would expect them to treat your (external) customers – teach by example.

Step Two: Refocus the organisation's very purpose – putting the customer at the centre of the organisation changes how you do everything. Can you afford not to?

In your 'customer initiative programme', you and your staff need to ask the following:

- ☐ Why do customers buy the product at all?
- ☐ Why do they buy it from you?
- ☐ How are you different from the competition?

☐ How will the customer benefit from this difference?
☐ What problem are you solving?
☐ What service levels do you expect to deliver?
☐ What service levels do the customers get?
☐ What are the minimum acceptable service standards?
☐ Do you understand and do you give basic courtesy?

Checklist – serving the customer: questions to ask yourselves
Companies endlessly claim to be in the business of customer service. How many actually take the time to find out what customer service really means? Nine times out of ten the service specification (if there is one!) is defined not by the customer but by the service provider.

Ask the following of everyone in the organisation:

☐ What does your brand represent?
☐ What do your customers expect from you?
☐ How do they expect to be treated?
☐ How far do you exceed their expectations?
☐ What do you do when you fail to meet these expectations?
☐ Are your processes, systems and front-line people set up to give the sort of service that the 'promise' suggests?
☐ Is there a 'promise'?

How to keep customers for life

Any initiative to 'put the customers first' must be underpinned by the following assumptions:

1 Reward them – make it feel good to do business with you; let them know what great service they are getting.
2 Forget about selling – people love to buy; they hate to be sold *at*!
3 People buy only good feelings and solutions to problems.
4 Keep asking, 'What's the unmet need?', 'How are we doing?', 'How can we do better?'

We are talking about shifting the way you work – to move away from a focus on transactions and towards becoming a business built on relationships. All this takes persistence and passion!

Customer focus is not 'just another initiative': it is possibly the only way forward!

Prove you care – a thirteen-point plan

- Have a written document outlining your principles of customer service.
- Establish systems that focus on service superiority.
- Measure and reward.
- Passion for the value of excellent service must run through every part of the business.
- Be genuinely committed to being better than anyone else in the industry.
- Be sure you all pay close attention to the customer.
- Ask questions of the customer and *listen* to the answers.
- Stay in touch with customers.
- Be alert to trends.
- Share information with the front line.
- Recognise the human as well as the business relationship.
- Invest in systems that make your whole business sound friendly.
- Remember: what customers value most are attention, dependability, promptness and competence.

Benefits of a customer-care programme

Case study

Lumina, a French hi-fi retailer, was watching repeat sales tail off compared with previous years. Staff were tired, and the customers had commented on this. Pierre Antoinette, the owner, knew that focusing on the customer would improve business performance. He knew that the organisation would then give the customers what they really want. Success would come if they could decide which customers they wanted and then customise the service to fit those customers particular needs.

'We realised that the most profitable customers were those with big budgets who wanted a very individual service: auditions in their own home (or office) environment, a whole-system approach to cover all sound and vision needs in the building: music, TV, video, radio, all synchronised and co-ordinated to reflect personal needs.'

Pierre brought together his key managers and staff for an 'awayday'. He explained the need to move from being a generalist hi-fi retailer to becoming a specialist in exclusive, bespoke set-ups. The staff rallied around, recognising that the new focus would make the business unique and would allow them to specialise on a particular customer segment. This would be more rewarding personally and for the business.

The discipline of putting a specific customer type first allowed systematic planning and clearer priorities. All of this helped business performance. Focusing on customer needs changed the whole outlook of the business as it reviewed all its functions in a new light. The business promoted its specialist, unique skills to specific potential customers.

By focusing on customer needs, Lumina was able to establish a competitive advantage. Staff focused on what was really required of, and from, them by the customer as well as the business! 'We strive constantly to increase the value that customers receive and they love it.'

Checklist: customer charter – what they expect from you

- [ ] Don't waste our time.
- [ ] Remember who we are.
- [ ] Make it easy for us to buy from you (order and procure service).
- [ ] Make sure your service delights us!
- [ ] Customise your products and service for me!

Checklist: employee charter – what they expect when working for you

Give me:

- [ ] Interesting work
- [ ] Opportunities to use my skills
- [ ] Some challenge (but not too much!)
- [ ] Personal and professional growth opportunities
- [ ] Some form of self-satisfaction
- [ ] Some variety (but not too much!)
- [ ] Recognition by peers and others
- [ ] Security of employment and a decent wage

Frequently asked questions

Q. The only things that motivate staff are fear and greed. Are you proposing that I share my business with my staff?

A. Yes – you cannot do it all on your own. You must get your staff to buy into what you are trying to do. To have an adversarial relationship with your staff is very short-sighted. It is much easier (for you and, more importantly, for your customers) for you to work with rather than against your staff.

Q. You can never satisfy all your customers. If you bend over backwards to help them, they will simply expect more from you next time, and probably at a lower price. Do you agree that your approach may work on paper but not in the real world?

A. No – these tactics are very much from the real world. In the same way that you would return to a restaurant that made a special effort to delight you, so it can be with your customers. Customer delight is the name of the game. Most buying is not based on price alone but on relationships. People buy from people and the more 'people' aspects that you put into the package, then the greater chance you have of making yourself look different and memorable.

Q. How do you start a customer-care plan?

A. Give the opportunity to your staff. They probably know many of your customers better than you do. They probably have insights into what the customers like and dislike. Get them together and get them to go through the 'serving the customer' checklist above, and then the thirteen-point plan, also listed above. You will be amazed at what they come up with.

Summary

Get your people involved in your focus on marketing. This is no easy task and requires putting in place a systematic programme. Everyone must see the business through the customers' eyes.

CHAPTER NINE

Leaders as band leaders and surfers

Here we use the concept of the business leader as jazz-band leader or surfer! This is no substitute for a thorough examination of leadership as you would find in a dedicated human-resources book, but it does provide a good grounding for our overview.

The orchestra conductor has often been cited as the perfect metaphor of a leader, because the conductor is capable of creating harmony from an enormously complex team. In the army, as well as in business, campaigns are regularly referred to as having to be 'orchestrated' to describe the complexity.

Leading the music – and the beat goes on . . .

The need to manage complexity seems to become more and more important. This pressure is so great that maybe the skills of the jazz-band leader are now required more than the skills of the classical orchestra leader.

In essence, classical music is 'old school', where you know what is going to happen in the end. In jazz, anything can happen, a bit like the modern business environment.

Technically, jazz involves taking a theme, taking it to bits within a rhythmic framework, and putting that back together such that two plus two equals five – you have more than you started with. The great jazz leader has to be thoroughly schooled in the fundamentals, yet possess an absolute technical competence, and also be able to improvise on a theme. The crucial skill of modern management is this ability to improvise on a theme; this is what separates the classical from the jazz leader.

The ability to improvise is crucial: it is this ability that enables the leader to develop and understand patterns as they unfold. For most leaders there is no real score or script. The leader is given a theme around which he or she must work and improvise.

The metaphor of jazz is a rich one. You need only to think of some of the great jazz musicians of the later half of the twentieth century to see the similarities. Great names such as Duke Ellington, Miles Davis, John Coltrane, Gil Evans, Keith Jarrett, and Stephane Grappelli took traditional themes and ways of working and pushed them to the limit – as with all innovative work, some of it didn't seem to make so much sense to the 'mainstream'.

However, years of expanding what were originally narrowly defined parameters have opened up new possibilities for the players (and their customers, the audience).

Ellington, Davis, Coltrane and Grappelli can be seen as examples of the expansion of the 'traditional' way of doing things; compare them with one of the more innovative modern business leaders, say, Tom Peters, classically trained and thoroughly grounded in the fundamentals of their profession.

The Richard Bransons and Anita Roddicks are equally grounded, although their learning may not be quite so formal (compare Miles Davis or John Coltrane for the less classically trained jazz players).

Both management and jazz leaders should be great team players (the Dave Brubeck Quartet was together for sixteen years). Both types of leader need to be great innovators and have a passion for the success of the team that is matched only by the compassion for the team. Humility is shown in giving credit to the team.

What counts is the leader and his/her ability to take the whole further, beyond existing, safe boundaries, to improvise and learn continuously. To learn you have to make mistakes, but the key is to learn from those mistakes.

Management-speak and jazz-speak do merge. The role of the leader is to achieve the task – after all, this is why the group exists. The other main role is to maintain effective relationships.

Management and jazz leaders are committed to achieving results through people. Their main objectives will be to:

- Gain the commitment and co-operation of the team
- Get the group into action to achieve some kind of agreed objectives
- Make the best use of the skills, energies and talents of the team

Successful leaders need to harness and satisfy the needs of the task, the group and the individuals to be successful.

Case study

A lovely example of the difference between (visionary) leadership and (getting-things-done) management has emerged as a number of critics suggest that Paul McCartney rather than John Lennon was in some respects the creative leader of the Beatles.

Yoko Ono is quoted as springing to her dead husband's defence: 'John did not make the phone calls, he was not on that level as a leader – he was on the level of a spiritual leader … He was the visionary and that is why the Beatles happened.'

Will future musicologists view Sir Paul as little more than an organiser with a good telephone manner basking in the reflected glory of Lennon's genius? What a wonderful portrayal of the difference between the leader and the manager! Or, rather, the point is that together they were amazingly successful – a successful team needs both sets of skills.

As manager or owner of a business, you cannot do it all on your own. You have to have the support and assistance of your team to grow the business. In the top ten problems that face businesses, recruiting key staff comes right at the top along with finding customers, well ahead of raising finance, interest rates and red tape.

You need to be able to delegate. Employing people enables you to increase your overall capabilities and competencies. It also means that you progressively spend more time managing the people and less time 'doing the business'. So, a balance has to be found between your own psychological needs (what you want to do) and the needs of the business (what you should do)! There are plenty of excellent books that will help you sort out the staff issues.

Case study

MPT, the data-collection and data-handling agency, took the senior management team away to consider slipping staff morale. This focused the MD's mind on the benefits to be gained from better staff motivation and involvement. As a consequence of the meeting, it was agreed that a series of policies were to be introduced to deal systematically with the waning morale. 'Initiatives' were brought in to tackle the following issues:

- An appraisal system and a 'dismissal' system were designed by the staff to reflect their concerns and professional development needs.

- Training – internal courses were set up for all levels of research and data-handling staff; one of the general managers was appointed to research training opportunities; individual training plans were written; training budget per department was allocated.

- Communication – each department now has a monthly 'communication day' to improve upward and downward communication. All key staff see outline budgets and financial performance on a quarterly basis.

- Feedback – a biannual survey of our staff attitudes to the company was commissioned (through an outside agency), which is reported back to staff, 'warts and all'.

- Social activities – a social committee was established, jointly funded by staff and company, to arrange a wide range of social events.

MPT's Daniel Elmfield, makes it all sound so easy: 'As a result we now have excellent staff, and one of the lowest levels of staff turnover in the industry.'

Leaders as surfers – the surfer's guide to management

The large business is like the sluggish supertanker; smaller businesses are altogether smaller and nimbler vessels – the skills of the supertanker captain are fundamentally different from those of the surfer.

Using the analogy of a boat moving swiftly down a river, David Storey's *Ten Percenters* report recognises that a fast-growing business is like a boat moving quickly in a fast current in a river.

One of two things was going on in the growing businesses: either there was a capable crew or the boat was backed by a strong current. Or both. On the whole, the entrepreneurs had placed their boat, their business, in a very fast current. The management of the crew is not as crucial as the placing of the boat in the right current (being in the right place at the right time).

The fast-growing companies were almost always in growing niche markets (the strong current). The crews were not, however, uniformly organised. Indeed, a number of the crews were euphemistically described as 'not well managed'. This analogy with water helps us to understand the situation and give us clues as to how to behave.

To extend the analogy, most growing companies should take on the attributes of the surfer. A good surfer has skills that the entrepreneur should also have.

- **Surfers come in all shapes and sizes but the really good ones are obsessive.** Go to Cornwall and you'll see the beginners, the vulnerable and the plodders floundering on the water's edge – the 'real surfers' are far from the beach taking the big waves. Likewise, real entrepreneurs look for the big opportunities.

- **Surfers look after their own fitness and equipment.** Real surfers have their favourite boards, board wax, wet suits and equipment. They know how much they depend on their own wits when out alone. They may look relaxed but they take their sport very seriously: one bad move could be fatal! In business, you must always be prepared for trouble.

- **Surfers are always looking for the next wave.** They constantly scour the sea for the next wave – they look ahead, behind, beside, above and below for any clues as to where the next wave will come from. They read the currents, undertows and rips of each beach. They are aware and responding to minute changes in the weather and the immediate environment (including other surfers) – they recognise that their lives might depend on their ability to understand and respond to that environment. So, while they may try to plot a general course, their real interest (they have a nose for it) is in looking for the next big wave. In commerce, concentrate on tomorrow's as well as today's business.

■ **Good surfers are able to catch waves that others miss.** They see, or rather they make, opportunities where others see none; they always seem to be in the right place at the right time. Entrepreneurs spot opportunities (that some others don't see) and act upon them.

■ **Good surfers don't take risks but rather they take calculated risks.** Like good strategists, surfers recognise the need not to try to take every wave: they specialise, concentrate and focus their efforts to be as effective as possible – Pareto's 80/20 Principle (the law of the trivial many and the critical few) applies to the waves as much as it does in the commercial environment.

■ **Success and failure go hand in hand; the more you practise the luckier you seem to get.** It takes practice to be able to tackle the big waves successfully: you start on the nursery beaches and work your way up to the really challenging waves. The big waves are not for the faint of heart: big excitement also means big danger! Business must grow through a life cycle – don't punch above your weight unless you are willing to take the risk!

■ **Good surfers make it look so easy.** Kelly Slater makes surfing through the rolling barrels of Tenerife and Hawaii look so very easy. Do not kid yourself – years of practice, hard work and learning from your mistakes are required before you can make it look so easy. The more you practise, the easier it gets.

■ **Spurts and fallbacks are a reality for even the good surfer.** The environment is not smooth. There are short-lived surges for the surfer to conquer – the skill is to be able to spot trends, and harness your own strength to capitalise on often short-term movements. Invest your energy to live to fight another day!

■ **Relative power.** Like most growing business, the surfer lacks power relative to the waves (market). Surfers are often pushed and buffeted and seem to be as likely to go backwards as forwards – energy must be used to leverage your own power effectively. Use the power of the current and the wave to your own advantage.

■ **Exploiting the environment.** The skill is in recognising the surges and not being thrown by them. The good surfer exploits the wave, no matter how temporary the advantage may appear

> to be. Watch surfers as they paddle out to sea against the waves – no unnecessary energy is expended. Excellent managers do the same.
>
> ■ **Flexibility and responsiveness.** The surfer is able to tap hidden depths of physical and mental flexibility and responsiveness. The sea is unpredictable. You need to be able to react to whatever the elements might throw at you. And so it is when you're running a business.

Excellent surfers are preoccupied with finding the ultimate wave; they are preoccupied with planning to get to their endpoint while being obsessed with the surrounding environment; they are aware of how the constituent parts (surfer, board, wax and suit) must work together to achieve the 'whole'.

Much research makes the implicit assumption that any mention of teamwork refers to civilised, liberal, human-resource (HR) management practices – i.e. good teamwork means management by consensus. This assumption is being proven to be flawed – many growing businesses demonstrate less than contemporary approaches to the management of the team.

You need only to look at teams under stress – in the armed forces, for instance – to realise that the business-school version of teamwork (consensus and agreement) is not effective in crisis. 'Liberal' HR management may be appropriate for managers, but not for leaders; and high-growth businesses are certainly led rather than managed!

Strong, decisive, judgmental control-and-command-type leadership is what is required in turbulent weather (by the surfer and many growing businesses). There is still a place for those managers I call the TUBs (Total and Utter Bastards) – I'd hate to have one babysit my children but they know how to get things done in times of crisis. How they fare in the long run is another matter!

Real entrepreneurs are born surfers

Entrepreneurs, like surfers, are driven by specific psychological attributes – some might describe these as flaws. Many have an all-consuming need to prove something to themselves and to others.

Many suffer deep down from low self-esteem; some are profoundly insecure, always trying to prove that they can do better than the opinion that they hold of themselves.

The standard definitions of entrepreneurs could be a description of a surfer – they are 'bounce-back' people with a powerful desire to achieve. They do not get distracted by either success or failure: they just plough on, never satisfied and constantly in fear of 'being found out'. Often after one success, they need to do it again to prove it was not a fluke. Failure is seen as confirming inner fears, but they do not give up. Instead they pick themselves up and attempt to show that they can get it right a second time. Many do not care about anything other than the business in hand – it can be like a drug.

Checklist – leadership

The leadership checklist based on the work of John Adair examines the three overlapping needs of the fields of leadership: the task, the team and the individuals.

1 The task
   a) What needs to be done and why?
   b) What results have to be achieved?
   c) What problems have to be overcome?
   d) Is this a straightforward or an ambiguous problem, or is this a crisis situation?
   e) What is the time scale?
   f) What pressures will be exerted on you?
2 The team
   a) What is the composition of the team?
   b) How well is it organised?
   c) Do the team members work well together?
   d) What will they want out of this?
   e) How can you gain and maintain their commitment?
   f) How will they respond to various leadership styles or approaches?
3 The individuals
   a) What are the strengths and weaknesses of each team member?

b) What sorts of things are likely to motivate them?

c) What sort of leadership style will they respond to best?

Checklist – achieving high levels of motivation

To achieve high levels of motivation, take the following steps:

1 Set and agree demanding goals.
2 Provide feedback on performance.
3 Be clear about what behaviours will be celebrated.
4 Design jobs so that people feel a sense of value, pride, ownership and accomplishment.
5 Reward properly (both financially and non-financially).
6 Train, develop, guide and coach.
7 Set clear goals and opportunities for the future.

Frequently asked questions

Q. Why is it that, as I have more and more staff, I seem to spend less and less time doing my work?

A. The art of being a great leader is being able to get the people beneath you to do what you want them to do. It takes time and skill to master this art. As the business grows you need to recognise that your old job may well have become redundant for you. Leading the business is too important to be left to chance. Your job is to direct and to lead while you can employ people to manage the day-to-day operations.

Q. So should a leader be all 'leadership by agreement' or should you be dictatorial and totalitarian in your approach?

A. Adjust your leadership style to fit the situation. There are times when decisive action needs to be taken; do not be afraid to be assertive in what you want and how and when you want something. But be aware that this kind of behaviour works only in a crisis or time-constrained situation.

Summary

Business leaders cannot do everything on their own. You need to recognise that your people must be allowed to fly – you must allow them to make mistakes (as long as they learn). Your business needs its people to bring their enthusiasm, commitment and energy to their jobs. This is best done by leading without limiting – a risky strategy! Successful people management is not always the domain of the consensual manager. Different situations require different management styles. In the fast-moving business environment, it is often necessary to be decisive.

CHAPTER TEN

Running the business

To grow a business you need to spend time working on and not simply working in the business. A well-functioning board should be the 'business brain'. Few directors, especially in a growing business, understand what they are meant to do when they are a director – they must understand their roles and duties for the business to be effective. You should run the business rather than the let business run you!

An effective business needs people working *in* the business, making and selling its wares. It also needs people working *on* the business, planning for the future and taking an overview on what is really going on.

Most small businesses do not work. It is as simple as that.

The majority of small businesses are run by owner-managers who behave like victims. They endlessly grumble about overheads, staff and so forth. They beat themselves up and their businesses will never generate the profits that they dream of earning. There is a simple reason for this mass failure of so-called entrepreneurs – they spend all their time *in* the business and not *on* the business.

To explain where my argument is coming from, I would like to expand on the various levels of what is sometimes called entrepreneurship.

Entrepreneurial seizure

Here is the story of a typical small-time entrepreneur.

A perfectly competent garage mechanic or a management consultant or a painter and decorator is employed by their boss. At some point they realise that they are being charged out for more than they are worth. They have a split second of original thought, when they say something to the effect of, 'I could run a business and do it much better than my boss.'

This blinding flash of inspiration is the beginning of the end. From now on they can think, dream and talk of nothing else other than when they run their own business.

Almost hypnotised and in a trancelike state they start a relentless persual of self-employment. To them self-employment represents freedom from the slavery and mastery of their boss over their working life.

The hero of our tale believes that the future will be paved with gold. What they usually do not realise is that being a competent craftsman or technician is one thing. But being a competent manager of a business is something entirely different.

Our hero ends up buying himself or herself a job for life. Nobody disputes their particular technical skill (be it architect, doctor, artist, roofer) but they simply do not have the skills to run a business. They have no real expertise in the skills of managing people, pricing, tax, banks, cash flow, accounts and all the various skills required to run a business.

As a consequence they end up as the proverbial headless chicken. They work hard but not always effectively. They become dependent on others (staff, customers, bankers) while they thought they would become independent. They go to their local bar and mumble and groan about how the business runs their life and how tough things are.

The key to changing this state of affairs is to recognise that a business needs to be run – it needs to be managed. It needs to be planned and designed – things don't just happen. You need to spend more time working *on* your business and less time working *in* your business. That is the key to running a business rather than having the business run you.

What so many people seek self-employment to escape from (systems and structure) is often the very thing that small businesses need to put in place to give them the independence that they seek.

True entrepreneurs seek opportunities and try to make things happen – this can be done when you have a system that will manage and do the work ('minders' and 'grinders').

The successful entrepreneur is more than a technician, more than a manager. Some self-employed, like the caterpillar growing into the butterfly, go through several stages – technician to manager to entrepreneur – shedding their metaphorical skin at each stage as they develop on to the next. Some combine all three. Some never progress beyond the stage of technician.

The central issue here is that you can spend your time only once. Every hour you spend working *in* your business is an hour that you are not spending working *on* it. The trade-off is that you either work on today's business or you work on tomorrow's business. Too much time on tomorrow's business and you have no income – to much time on today's business and you will fail to plan for tomorrow.

One of the fundamental skills of the successful businessperson is the ability to spend time planning and designing the future, not just building it!

Case study

Lewis Hunter set up Hunter, the commercial fridge repairers, from home in 1978 based on his experience as an engineer in the refrigeration industry. By 2000, Hunter had a turnover in excess of £1 million, employed 21 staff and had plans to double turnover within twelve months.

'Growth followed a natural progression,' says Lewis. 'Back in the early years we took on extra staff whenever a customer asked for service engineers outside my area of expertise. For instance, in to service catering equipment. And now the company has become a one-stop servicing centre.'

Despite the growth, the business had no strategic or marketing plans. 'We were lucky,' says Lewis. 'Work came in through the door. But we realised that we needed to develop the company structure to ensure its survival.'

The business has now sorted its IT and operational sides. Lewis spends more time working on the business. He takes on more of the forward planning and marketing roles (business planning, forecasting, setting strategies, developing the brand for the future) as well as dealing with key customers and their future needs. This leaves Mike, his second-in-command, in charge of the engineering side.

Stepping back and understanding the business has enabled Lewis to develop and plan the growth of the business. Now Lewis says, 'If I can do it in my home town it can be duplicated elsewhere.' He is looking to increase turnover by £1.4 million over twelve months.

Lewis's story is an example of applying a system to the company. He has worked *on* the business, and has stopped firefighting and working *in* the business. He has recognised the need to build the organisation, seeing the company itself as the product of his work.

Lewis put into action what we call the XOX formula. With a poor system, it doesn't matter how good your people are, you still get ordinary results in the end. The system will beat the people every time:

An ordinary system (O) + extraordinary people (X) = ordinary results (O).

On the other hand, with an extraordinary system, ordinary people can produce extraordinary results: extraordinary system (X) + ordinary people (O) = extraordinary results (X).

The best example of XOX in practice is a major fast-food chain, where hundreds of outlets have got not particularly well-educated young adults delivering an identical product all over the world. This is a marvel when you think that many restaurants find it hard enough to get a cup of coffee to your table.

Your mission is to put a system in place that reduces error and guarantees that your business delivers on its promise consistently. Such systems can be cloned and replicated to grow your business.

Case study

Wild Oats had been a great success as a relaxed eating house for health-minded locals. Customers loved the food and ambience apart from one small problem. They never actually knew what exactly they were going to get. Using three different cooks and seven part-time serving staff, Wild Oats demonstrated no consistency in terms of what a salad looked like, or how big a portion should be. Definitions of what a curry should look or taste like were equally unpredictable.

While this bohemian approach to business amused some, it actually upset a lot of their customers, who concluded that such randomness of cooking methods might extend to kitchen hygiene. More importantly, Donald Jakes, the owner, could not predict how long food would take to be served and quite what the attitude of the staff would be when the food got there.

Donald decided that enough was enough. He put in place what was at first a severe regime, defining standards and qualities that everyone had to work to. Standard recipes and portion sizes were issued. A 'standard' acceptable way of serving was determined.

While the restaurant may not have been so much fun for a while, the customers relished the consistency and started to recognise a more consistent style in the business's product. Apart from one member of staff who walked out, the rest ended up feeling happier with their jobs. They knew what was expected of them and they knew what was and what was not acceptable. Says one, 'In the old days it seemed like it was us who were making up the rules as we went along. It was fun for a while, but it seems better this way, and now we have just as much fun, if not more, because we know what's expected of us.'

Donald had worked *on* the business and had concentrated on putting in systems, which were subsequently copied at his second restaurant. Although it was tough for Donald to bite the bullet and put in place stuffy rules and regulations, everyone benefited in the long run.

Directing or managing?

Many small business directors are given the title as a matter of course. Legally, anyone who acts as a director is considered to be a director of the company.

So how many directors or boards of directors actually know what the difference between a director and a manager is? You ask what the role of a director is and most start mumbling about the board and responsibility for the business and share options and so forth. It is as if you were meant to absorb the job description by osmosis when you are given the role. As with parenting, you are not given a manual and most make it up as you go along.

As working definitions, managers look after the day-to-day affairs. Most managers are glorified supervisors. Directors, on the other hand, are responsible for all aspects of the business (as well as for the performance of their own areas of responsibility), and its future direction.

The role of the board is fundamental to the growth of the business.

The roles of the board

The board's duties have been clarified in recent years and the four roles of the board are:

1 Policy formulation
2 Strategic thinking
3 Supervision of management
4 Accountability

They still present us with what can be described as some fundamental 'directorial dilemmas'.

- The board must simultaneously be entrepreneurial and drive the business forward while keeping it under prudent control.
- The board is required to be sufficiently knowledgeable about the workings of the company to be answerable for its action and yet to stand back from the day-to-day management and retain an objective view.
- The board must be sensitive to the pressures of the short term and yet be informed of the broader trends and competition.
- The board is expected to be focused on the commercial needs of the business while acting responsibly towards its employees, business partners and society in general.

The board is the business brain – it links the short term and the long term; it links the external and the internal perspective.

Simple Learning Board Model

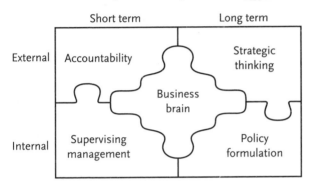

Source: B Garratt 97

It is an effective board that will let a business grow and flourish. Conversely, an incompetent board will probably destroy a business. Hence the apt title of Bob Garratt's book is *The Fish Rots from the Head*.

Get your business's brain sorted out. Without clarity of leadership, focus, vision, and mission, your business will die. One of the real challenges for the growing business is to appoint and run an effective board that leads the business – working *on* and not *in* the business. How much time do you spend working on your business?

Frequently asked questions

Q. Where do I find out how to be a director?

A. Go to your local business support agency, accountant or lawyer and find out your legal responsibilities. More importantly, get your directors to start behaving like a team that is directing the business rather than an aimless group of people.

Q. When should I appoint a finance director?

A. The appointment of FD normally assumes that the business is big enough to support the salary and associated costs of a director focusing on financial matters. Active FDs start appearing only with 35 employees or more, although there are no fixed rules. Financial institutions like to see an FD, as this suggests that the finances of the business are the responsibility of a qualified expert.

Q. I'd much rather spend my time setting up lots of businesses than run one business for ages. What should I do?

A. This is a 'serial entrepreneur' or a 'dreamer' asking this question. You can move on to a new business project only when the first one is secure and can afford to be managed by a paid employee. If you get your business model right, then you should be able to leave the business to run itself. It requires a cool and calculated approach to business to be able to set up the shop and walk away. Alternatively, you need to have confidence in the model and the team to whom you are handing it over. One of the key limits to business growth is the owner's inability to relinquish control.

Q. What's the difference between being a board director of a small business and being the director of a big business?

A. In a small business the director is responsible to the owner, who is probably working in the business. In a large business you are responsible to the shareholders, who can vote you in or out of office. Aside from that, it is simply a question of scale and resources.

Q. I have been invited to be the director of a local business employing seventy staff. I have worked there for a couple of years and I need some advice. Where should I go?

A. Go to your lawyer and to your accountant. Get professional advice.

Q. I've been invited to be the non-executive director of a close friend's business. Is it worth it?

A. The role of the NED is becoming more and more important. The NED does not work in the business but works at board level, usually on an occasional basis. The advantages for the business are that the NED has a helicopter view of the company and should be able to bring his/her experience to bear in a positive way. As an NED, you need to look at your 'package' in terms of responsibilities and payment.

Summary

If you seriously wish to grow your business, then you need to spend more time working *on* the business and less time working *in* the business. The role of the director is crucial to the growth of the business. Do you really know what is expected of you and your fellow directors?

CHAPTER ELEVEN

Sort finance

There are some key fundamentals that you must come to terms with in managing the finances of your business. Ignoring these numbers makes the business vulnerable. This chapter will not tell you how to 'do finance' in your growing business. It will not make you into an accountant. But it will focus on the key financials that you must pay attention to.

This chapter will give you pointers to what you must look at in your business. If some of these fundamental concepts make no sense to you then you must enrol for a good practical hands-on programme on finance. You can kid plenty of people about your financial shrewdness (and most MDs are pretty good at looking as if they know what they are talking about) but a growing business must be managed by a team that does understand the financial implications of its growth plans.

At its simplest, whenever you see the word 'growth' you can substitute the word 'cash'. Growth equals cash. In fact, growth normally means 'cash out' of your business. Do not be under any illusions about that.

It is easy to get wooed by the arguments in favour of growth and increased turnover and staff and new premises. In fact, I am teased by some accountants that my enthusiasm for business growth is bordering on the irresponsible. They argue that while the marketing brain will see all the opportunities, and the various 'signs of success', the reality is often somewhat grimmer.

An eagerness to grow goes hand in hand with what could be described as a 'cash-flow delusion' – a belief that, by your doubling turnover, suddenly people will pay you more quickly and you'll be able to pay out more slowly. A fantasy!

So what should be done?

First and foremost, understand that the price of growth, even profitable growth, is paid in terms of cash flow.

Maister's checklist

I have looked to David Maister's profit-improvement checklist as the place to seek assistance. Time and time again, this checklist is not adhered to and the penalty for ignoring it is severe.

It is a list of profitability tactics (in descending order of impact on profit health):

1 Raise the selling price
2 Lower the cost of sales
3 Focus on the profitable lines and drop the underperformers
4 Increase volume
5 Lower overheads

Tactics 1 and 2

The first two items, selling price and cost of sales, are all about gross profit margin. Beware of 'GP drift'. So often, business is booming (in terms of turnover) and you forget to look at gross profit. Assumptions are made about pricing and job costing; you use your usual suppliers and forget to renegotiate prices and terms of trade. Look for any fat that you may have allowed to creep in and eliminate it, now.

You can earn higher prices by specialising and by adding more value to the customer (doing it better). Or you can use marketing to get better contracts (do it better or do it nicer). Likewise, you can improve your business efficiency (do it faster or do it cheaper). You must develop systems to speed up how you deliver value to the customer.

Below are two tables. You can use the tables to calculate how much your sales volume must change to compensate for a change in price (and still keep the same gross profit margin). Conversely you could use these charts to estimate the impact of changes in gross profit percentages.

Table to calculate percentage sales volume decrease as a result of price increases at various gross-margin per-cent levels to maintain same gross margin

per cent price increase	Existing percentage gross margin								
	5	10	15	20	25	30	35	40	50
⬇	Percentage unit/volume decrease to generate same gross margin								
2.0	29	17	12	9	7	6	5	5	4
3.0	37	23	17	13	11	9	8	7	6
4.0	44	29	21	17	14	12	10	9	7
5.0	50	33	25	20	17	14	12	11	9
7.5	60	43	33	27	23	20	18	16	13
10.0	67	50	40	33	29	25	22	20	17
15.0	75	60	50	43	37	33	30	27	23

Table to calculate percentage sales volume increase as a result of price reductions at various gross-margin per-cent levels to maintain same gross margin

per cent price reduction	Existing percentage gross margin								
	5	10	15	20	25	30	35	40	50
⬇	Percentage unit/volume increase to generate same gross margin								
2.0	67	25	15	11	9	7	6	5	4
3.0	150	43	25	18	14	11	9	8	6
4.0	400	67	36	25	19	15	13	11	9
5.0		100	50	33	25	20	17	14	11
7.5		300	100	60	43	33	27	23	18
10.0			200	100	67	50	40	33	25
15.0				300	150	100	75	60	43

Case study

RHT, the outside-catering company who specialise in pop festivals, were turning over £950,000 with a gross margin of 40 per cent (after all direct costs). Judi, the owner was considering the impact of price changes. The tables clearly indicated the following:

> ■ A price increase of 4 per cent would mean that she would generate the same gross margin (£s) even if sales volumes fell by 9 per cent.
>
> ■ A price increase of 5 per cent would mean that she would generate the same gross margin (£s) even if sales volumes fell by 11 per cent.
>
> ■ A price increase of 10 per cent would mean that she would generate the same gross margin (£s) even if sales volumes fell by 20 per cent.

Judi says, 'I decided to put prices up by 10 per cent on the assumption that trade may slow down a little, but the benefits would go straight down to the bottom line – I reckon that most punters are not too price-sensitive within reason, and we are currently seen to be on the cheap side.

'The gamble paid off. Volumes did drop but only by a small amount, later calculated to be about 5 per cent. The net effect was beneficial to all – less activity, less output, greater profits and better cash flow.'

Judi's story tells us to be brave with our pricing. It is rarely clever to lower your prices because of the damage to your bottom line – you end up being busier and with less profit per transaction.

Tactic 3

Once the GP drift has been sorted out, then attention can be turned to profitable lines. Where do you make the real profit in the business? Which products/lines generate the real profit? And which activities generate no profit?

Focus on doing more with the highly profitable and you must deal with the underperformers – drop the underperforming products and services; drop the unprofitable customers.

When looking at the profitables, look for Pareto's 80/20 principle – 80 per cent of outputs (profit) will be generated by 20 per cent of inputs (customers/products/effort). This is the principle of the trivial many and the critical few, which says that most of your effort is a waste of time. Deal with the critical few and don't accept the excuses such as 'nonprofitable work is required to cover overheads' or other such nonsense.

Tactic 4

Only when you have sorted out your GP drift and your underperformers can you look at increasing volume. To do so earlier would put you in a position of becoming even busier and yet less profitable than you were becoming in any case.

Tactic 5

And, when the first four steps have been followed, then you can consider reducing overheads. To do so earlier sends all the wrong messages to your workforce – they do not appreciate downgrading their company cars and the damage to morale is immeasurable!

By lowering your overheads, you are improving efficiency again. Reducing support costs and resources and improving efficiency must be undertaken with care – otherwise any anticipated benefits may be outweighed by the proverbial 'false economies' and consequential backlash.

Cash and capital

Cash-flow statements

The growing business must understand the cash-flow and working-capital implications of its plans. Look at last year's cash-flow statement. If you don't know what I am talking about then find out about them now!

Cash-flow forecasts

Do not work on creating a realistic cash-flow forecast. Work on a pessimistic one. Things are never as good as expected – cash haemorrhages from a growing business and will drive many a profitable business into the bankruptcy courts.

Net Working Capital (NWC) Requirement

You probably won't find NWC Requirement in your tatty out-of-date accounting textbook but you need to know it.

Working capital is fundamental to growth. What we are looking at is how much fuel you have to burn to pay for growth. At its simplest, it will cost you at least twice as much to pay for twice as much turnover – remember that you normally pay for staff, stock etc. faster than you get paid. The consequence is that cash drains out of the business.

To calculate Net Working Capital Requirement, go to the profit-and-loss account and balance sheet and apply the following:

$$\frac{\text{Stock} + \text{trade debtors} - \text{trade creditors}}{\text{Sales}} \times 100 = \text{Working Capital Requirement (per cent)}$$

Gross Profit – Working Capital Requirement = Net Working Capital Requirement

So, the big question is: is your Working Capital Requirement bigger or smaller than your gross profit? If bigger than your gross profit, then you've got a problem.

Break-even point

You must know the break-even point of each profit centre. If you don't know what a break-even point is, then to quote the old board game, 'Do not pass GO, do not collect £200'. Please find out about your BEP now!

Case study

Graham and Green started 25 years ago with one shop in west London. Steady rather than explosive growth has seen the business grow into a chain of five shops, and the range extend from kitchen and basketware into clothes, accessories and lifestyle goods. The latest outlet to open was a mini-department store.

Antonia Graham, the founder, realised that sales in her shops were not generating enough profit. 'Everyone thought that we must be doing well because the range we carry is top end of the market. In fact, we have never been profitable enough to drive the sort of growth we wanted. We needed to turn the situation around.

'Because we had identified profitability as a key area to be looked at, we developed active financial management systems. In effect, this meant that the new financial reporting systems could create a platform for effective management action. Now we could break down profitability by shop and by line. This made a big impact on the decisions we were making; we could make informed choices and predict the outcomes. If we had done it a year earlier, then we would have made an awful lot more money.'

Case study

Business Systems UK's Stephen Thurston on finance: 'Money drives or strangles a business. You have to understand how to read your own profit-and-loss account. Know why it is so important to have access to financial figures, and why it is so important to budget. If you come from a sales background as I did, those are not your prime considerations. Taking control of the financial figures has allowed us to manage the growth of the business.'

Checklist – productivity audit

When examining your organisation's productivity, you should first look at your performance to date before considering what you are capable of doing. The following areas should be considered:

1 Actual performance compared with company standards and trends
2 Actual performance compared with other organisations (benchmarking)
3 Reasons for unsatisfactory performance, under the following headings:
   a) Planning, budgeting and control procedures
   b) Inefficient work methods and systems
   c) Inadequate use of work measurement
   d) Poor management

    e) Poorly motivated or badly paid staff

    f) Inadequate training

    g) Excessive waste

Checklist – detailed profit improvement

Financial

1 Analyse contribution and costs generated by profit centre (markets, products).

2 Assess the market for each product: is it growing/shrinking/static?

3 Analyse and explain variances between planned and actual performance in sales and costs.

4 Analyse key ratio variances and explain the deviations.

5 Remedy adverse trends.

6 Conduct a zero-based budget for next time frame (i.e. starting from scratch).

7 Tighten credit policies (main impact on cash-flow).

8 Set priorities for capital expenditure (main impact on cash-flow).

9 Reduce bad debts.

10 Create fast effective and useful management information.

Strategy

1 What business are you in?

2 What business should you be in?

3 What are you good at doing?

4 FiMO/RECoIL analysis.

5 Assess external threats and opportunities.

Marketing

1 Find out as much as possible about customers.

2 Identify potential for getting new customers.

3 Segment the market where this means you can reach more profitable customers.

4 Penetrate new markets if this can be done profitably.

5 Check the cost-effectiveness of all advertising and sales materials.

Product mix and development

1 Optimise your return on investment by redistributing resources appropriately.

2 Maximise product profitability:

- Cut high risk, high capital projects.
- Develop low-risk, low-cost products.
- Cut costs.
- Reduce inventory and stock.
- Reduce discounts.
- Increase prices.
- Eliminate unprofitable lines.

Sales

1 Improve hit ratio (contact-to-contract sale) of sales force by better controls and by incentives.

2 Focus on key accounts.

3 Eliminate unprofitable accounts.

4 Find/develop more high-volume accounts.

5 Improve the discount structure.

6 Provide incentives for customers to place larger orders.

7 Provide better sales team support.

8 Respond faster to customer enquiries.

Production

1 Decide where and what to cut/improve:

   a) Labour costs
   b) Manufacturing costs
   c) Development costs
   d) Inventory costs
   e) Material costs
   f) Operating costs
   g) Distribution costs
   h) Productivity

2 Conduct a cost-reduction exercise analysing value. Ask:

   a) Does its use contribute to value?
   b) Is its cost proportionate to usefulness?

c) Does it need all its features?

d) Is there a better option that will meet the intended use?

e) Can a usable part be made by a less costly method?

f) Can a standard and less costly part be used instead?

g) Will another dependable supplier provide it at less cost?

h) Can alternative and cheaper materials/components be used?

i) Can it be manufactured with the use of less skilled labour or less expensive machinery or equipment?

j) Can it be manufactured in such a way as to reduce the number of standard hours required?

k) Can its design be simplified to reduce manufacturing costs?

l) Can the tolerances or specification be modified to ease manufacture and/or reduce reject rates?

People

1 Identify the 'water walkers' and promote and reward them.

2 Identify the ineffective and remove them.

3 Introduce motivating payment schemes.

4 Encourage and train managers and supervisors to motivate their staff.

5 Improve the organisation and quality of working life to achieve better motivation.

Checklist – pricing strategy

- [ ] Set pricing objectives.
- [ ] Don't set prices by feel or by guesswork.
- [ ] Relate your price objectives to your marketing strategy, e.g.
    - [ ] To penetrate the market
    - [ ] To be seen as fair
    - [ ] To follow competitors
- [ ] See the price through the customers' eyes – be market and customer-oriented.
- [ ] Don't be obsessed with your past.
- [ ] Get a handle on the customer price sensitivity.
- [ ] Make sure your pricing yields profits (or recognise why and for how long you will carry a loss)

Frequently asked questions

Q. How can I increase prices? And by how much?

A. Customers are pretty tolerant of price increases, especially if you can demonstrate added value. The problem comes when you are selling what is, in effect, a commodity. For instance, there are standard prices in the building trades and many purchasing officers do literally buy on price. Then you need to consider whether you are in the right business. Or find ways of doing what you do better, cheaper or faster.

Q. What is the impact of increasing my prices?

A. Normally you will lose some customers but they tend to be customers who are more price sensitive (and often the customers whom you *want* to lose). Ironically, some customers are surprised that your prices haven't increased for so long! Use the price-margin charts to calculate how much business you can afford to lose before your actual gross profit reduces.

Q. How can I continue to have cash-flow crises although my accountant tells me that we are in profit?

A. Profit and cash are two separate and yet competing beasts. To grow a business you need more and more cash to feed your purchases of stock and staff. It is not unusual for staff and stock to be paid for within, say, seven days, yet customers may not pay you for over a month. The result is a working-capital crisis. The big order looks like the 'light at the end of the tunnel' – the reality is that it is an express train heading straight for you.

Q. How can I get better value from my accountant?

A. Demand to receive cash-flow statements and figures to explain your net working capital. Do not put up with an occasional discussion. Get value for money. Seek advice that will actually help you to run your business. Or leave your current accountant and find someone who is actually adding value to you and your business!

Q. Surely finance really is the engine of the business, isn't it?

A. Yes, and no. Finance is the most important issue in the business, but not at the cost of excluding all other factors (mar-

keting, operations, people). Finance is a consequence of
other activities but it is not the sole activity of the business.
Look at finance in its broad context. Do not allow the
finance function to become the policeman in the business –
get the finance function to facilitate and support the
smoother and more effective running of other parts of the
business.

Summary

Take control of the finances of your business. Apply basic tactics to
your money management. Do not leave the money management to
chance. You must get expert advice, support and training to assist
you in this perilous world that you live in!

CHAPTER TWELVE

Growth and balance

Business growth means more staff. More staff needs careful thought. Too many people at the wrong level and you become either too top- or bottom-heavy. And what about the consequences for staff development and motivation?

Most businesses seem to have a rather generic-looking mission statement. It's normally on the lines of something like this: 'To deliver outstanding/better/cheaper/faster things; to be a great and satisfying place to work; to have the financial success that we all deserve.'

To satisfy the triad of excellent service/product, excellent workplace, and excellent money is no mean task. The pursuit of any one objective potentially undermines the other two. And so there is always a compromise to be met between satisfying what David Maister calls 'service, satisfaction and success'. These differing goals seem to be pulling in opposing directions.

Many factors affect this triad of objectives, but the key issue is the ratio of staff at senior-middle-lower levels.

The levels can be described in several ways.

> - First level – the upper level, the directors, the brains, the experts, the 'finders' of work
> - Second level – the middle level, the managers, the 'grey hairs', the 'minders' of the work
> - Third level – the lower level, junior staff, doers, procedures people, the 'grinders' of work

This breakdown of work into the three levels of finders, minders and grinders appears in most businesses. The key is the balance between the three levels.

Some businesses sell their brains, their expert intellectual knowledge – clients buy the brains, the top level; some of the sophisticated design consultancies sell their senior designers as their key competence.

Some businesses sell their managers' skills – the grey hairs that have seen similar problems in the past and can apply themselves to the particular issues. Many larger consultancies sell their middle-level-sector familiarity and the ability to repackage previous work.

Some business sell the skills of their 'grinders', selling lots of repeatable tasks that the proverbial 'keyboard monkey' can easily do. Typically, call centres and processing centres focus on making money from these activities.

The implications

Different businesses will have a different ratio between the different levels. If your organisation is too fat at the bottom (too many 'grinders'), then there will be too few opportunities for promotion and workers will lose their motivation and enthusiasm. If people join your firm for a job then you do not need to worry about the lack of opportunity that you are making available. If, however, you are trying to provide a career, then you must create a pyramid that provides career-development opportunities.

Conversely, if it is too fat at the top then too many people will be being promoted and there will be too many chiefs and not enough Indians. The consequences for the wage bill could be catastrophic.

A typical design-studio fee structure shows up some simple insights into where the business makes its money.

Webbed Design's fee structure looks as follows:

Level	Number	Fee rate	Utilisation	Fee income*	Salary	Net contribution
Senior	2	£200	30%	£120,000	£100,000	£20,000
Middle	5	£100	70%	£140,000	£50,000	£90,000
Lower	25	£75	100%	£150,000	£20,000	£130,000

Total Fees (£):		Total Salaries (£):	
■ Senior	240,000	■ Senior	200,000
■ Middle	700,000	■ Middle	250,000
■ Lower	3,750,000	■ Lower	500,000
	4,690,000		950,000

*appropriate figures for a 38½-hour week

A quick look at the figures and several things are clear. First, in this business the real money is made by the grinders, the coders. The more of them you have, the more profitable will be the business. But how wide can you make the pyramid of power? And yet these people are already working flat out and the span of control cannot accommodate a wider base to the pyramid.

Second, as the business grows, many of today's grinders may want to do higher-level work – the company aspires to better-quality work and yet, as more and more of your business is done by the better-quality people, so the contribution falls.

Third, if a doubling in income will mean a doubling of the entire pyramid then twice as many seniors will be required, so the partners will not receive any additional income for the additional output that the firm is creating.

Case study

BJM, a market research agency, carries out surveys to help companies better understand their markets and the effectiveness of their marketing activities. In 1990 turnover was £4.4 million with minimal profits!

'Financial analysis of our cost base identified the benefits to be gained from a less top-heavy and expensive research staff,' says BJM's managing director. 'Our expansion was fuelled by underpinning the existing senior staff with inexperienced, less expensive graduates who we have trained. As a result, research salaries have come down from 23 per cent to 19 per cent of our costs, with the benefits falling to the bottom line.'

Checklist – controlling the business

If you want to exercise good control of the business you need to:

1   Plan what you aim to achieve.

2 Measure regularly what has to be achieved.
3 Compare actual with expected achievements from the plan.
4 Take action to exploit opportunities revealed by this information or to correct deviations from the plan.

Case study

Webbed Design was seeking to double in turnover and double in size from 25 to 50 programmers. Using the finders/minders/grinders model they realised that the business could find an additional 25 coders, but the business would also need an additional five managers and another two finders/directors at the senior level. The two existing senior finder/owners came to terms with the fact that doubling size would do little for their own wealth; new partners would take the profits from the new work!

They decided to redesign the business and its processes so that the business could become more profitable per director. In other words, each director did less fee-earning work but was responsible for an additional manager and five grinders. This trick put more money into the directors' pockets!

Case study

The two directors of the Greenwich Village fashion design company GV2 wanted to increase their workforce form fifteen to fifty. Using the pyramid model, they realised that they would need to introduce a layer of middle management to supervise the new recruits. They decided to employ the new managers and recognised that these new appointments would by definition change the way that the business would be run. They did the sums and felt that the trade-off between reduced profitability and higher market share (and turnover) was acceptable.

Case study

Whitby Bird & Company is a sixteen-year-old firm of consulting engineers specialising in engineering in the built environment, and particularly structures and services. It has offices in London, Manchester, Bath and Cambridge and employs nearly 300 people.

Consulting engineering firms often have a problem with the transfer of knowledge. Periods of growth are often linked to the actions of key senior individuals, partners. They learn how to perform in key client meetings, have the networks and can inspire the teams. Growth means the key individuals are spread more thinly and new people have to be introduced to the front line.

Whitby Bird & Company solved this problem by a management technique they call 'twinning'. It is all about bringing the young people forward early, so they can go to client meetings, begin to develop the network and run projects while learning from a more experienced colleague.

The business is made up of a series of work teams and the twinning approach is applied across the company. Teams are led by two people. 'It's the idea that two heads are better than one,' says one of the partners, Mike Crane. But at this level it has an additional advantage. When a team gets too busy, it can be sliced down the middle, like a double helix, and two more leaders can be brought in. 'Nobody feels they've gone from a position of being supported to unsupported,' says Mark Whitby. 'It's very healthy, you can stretch people in this way without them feeling too stretched.'

For Whitby Bird, this management system has allowed them to develop a common culture, to earn a reputation of being youthful and to achieve growth rates of 30 per cent per annum. These achievements have been acknowledged in the profession when they won the *New Civil Engineer*'s Engineer of the Year Award. The real benefit for Mike Crane, however, is 'the fact that we still feel fantastically excited about what we do after sixteen years; a fact supported by our staff retention levels'.

Checklist – overcoming problems of control

1 Decide what you want to control.
2 Decide how you are going to measure and review performance.
3 Use techniques such as ratio analysis to make comparisons and to identify variations and problems.

4 Set up a control system.
5 Manage by exception.

Conclusions

Notably for service firms, key decisions need to be made about the types of project that are undertaken. The types of project determine the shape of the pyramid. The shape of the pyramid affects the financial and the career development possibilities. The model suggests that the most money is to be made when the majority of work is done by the juniors and not by the senior staff; this increases the need to monitor all work carefully. This is an argument to affirm that senior staff must work *on* the business and not *in* the business.

Frequently asked questions

Q. So, what does all this mean to me?

A. As you grow you need to be aware of the development needs of your staff. If you do not offer them development opportunities then they may leave. In partnerships be careful not to chase increased turnover alone. You can double the size of your business (partners, managers, grinders, turnover) and end up with the same partner salary as before.

Q. What can I do with this pyramid concept?

A. Look at the shape of your business. How wide is the pyramid at the bottom? If you intend to grow the business, which parts of the pyramid will make you money? As your business develops will you start to change the emphasis as the type of work changes?

Q. What's the right shape for my business?

A. There is no right shape for one business – the shape depends on where you make the real contribution to the business. Just be aware of the consequences of the 'shape' that your business model seems to adopt. Can you alter the shape and so improve profitability? What is the shape of your competitors? Is your shape sustainable in the long run?

Summary

Be aware of growth for growth's sake. Most notably in service firms, you must be aware of the shape of the organisation and how you wish to grow that shape. Take time to plan the shape of your future business – start with the end in mind.

CHAPTER THIRTEEN

Habits of effectiveness

Various authors have put together guidelines on how to be more effective. Drawing upon parts of them all, there is an outline of the key tenets of being more effective. This can be applied to us as individuals, to us as business managers and even to the business itself. While some people find this kind of material a little 'touchy-feely', many more people find it inspiring. You can choose for yourself!

Much of the following chapter is derived and adapted from several key sources, including Andy Gilbert, Stephen Covey, Napoleon Hill, Rick Dobbins, Peter Thomson and Brian Tracy.

These habits are nothing stunningly original although they profoundly affect many readers.

When you consider the following habits of effectiveness you can apply them to:

> ■ Ourselves as (private) individuals
> ■ Ourselves as managers
> ■ The businesses in which you work

What are these habits?

What are referred to as 'habits' might also be called principles or laws. They have been brought together as a series of interconnecting principles that would increase your effectiveness. What makes them special is that they apply the basic principles of auditing and acting, to the way that you manage your life and your business.

There are two basic assumptions to the effectiveness doctrine. Number One is that you live in a land of plenty. If you believe that you live in a land of scarcity, then you will always be happy to beat your friends and colleagues. This concept of scarcity makes you very self-centred. Such behaviour ultimately does you no good because you are perceived as grasping and greedy and others may no longer wish to work with you for fear of being 'abused'.

For example:

 As a manager, you need to work in a supportive network.

As a business, you need to develop long-term alliances with customers and suppliers who trust you.

Assumption Number Two is the concept of the 'paradigm', the way that you see things. Perception is reality, until proven otherwise. Our perception (how we see things) determines what we think is going on (our reality). For instance, is the glass half full or is it half empty? Is reading this book a problem or a challenge? How you see things is determined by the colour of your spectacles (rose-tinted or otherwise) rather than how the reality actually is.

Armed with these two assumptions you can now proceed to look at the habits of effectiveness, largely based on the work of Dr Stephen Covey.

Habit One: take responsibility – be proactive

Habit One uses that terrible P-word, 'proactive'. Highly over-used, the concept, however, is valid. It is the easiest thing to refuse to take responsibility for what happens to us, as if you were but a small cork floating in the sea of life. However, this approach puts you 'out of control' and makes circumstances control your life rather than the other way around. Hope is not a method.

Victim language is a great example of people being controlled: 'I've got to', 'I must', and 'They said I have to'. Taking control of your life is often about having the strength to say 'no'.

For instance, as long as you feel you have to work with an old client who pays last year's fees, you feel that you are cheating on yourself. But if you decide to tell them that you will start charging this current year's fee rates you have made a decision to look after yourself and in effect taken control of the situation. You have decided that the principle is important enough and that you are prepared to suffer the consequences should they choose to stop working with you.

Research with elderly people discovered two interesting things. The first is that they regretted little of what they had done. The second is that they had lots of regrets about what they did not do. So, take control of your life!

Examples in practice

- As an individual, you are often not assertive enough about what you want, and hence feel abused.
- As a manager, you need to decide what needs to be done and take action accordingly.
- As a business, you need to decide what it is that you wish to do rather than wait and see what happens – you need to be decisive and not reactive.

Habit Two: decide what is important – starting with the end in mind

If you don't know where you are going then any road will do. You can't simply expect to live in house worth £350,000. Unless you're incredibly lucky, this will not just happen. But if you know what you want then you can put your mind to working towards it, and recognise the steps that need to be taken.

Decide your goals and be prepared to pay the price (in advance) – think strategically. If you know what the end point might be then you know what is important to you. Surely you should always do the things that are important! To work in any other way would be to waste time!

Examples in practice

- As an individual, you can choose which lifestyle you adopt for your family; going for a high income carries a cost for all, but how often do you audit whether you have got the right goal (if any) and how can you expect to arrive (or know if you have arrived) if you haven't mapped out your destination or route?

> ▪ As a manager, you need to make decisions about your career and future as well as what you are trying to achieve within the job.
>
> ▪ As a business you need to decide what you want to do – your goal will determine what you should be doing now – are you trying to be the biggest or the best or the friendliest or just satisfy your own needs or what?

Goals give a sense and a shape to all the things around you. You are able to consider whether you wish to do something in terms of whether it is helping you towards your goals or away from them.

Case study

Interaction was formed in 1990 to provide a professional service to the commercial office-interiors market. The two original founders/directors both had a common goal, one 'selling' the services and the other 'making it happen'.

The company grew steadily in the early years to a turnover of £2 million. Throughout the mid-1990s the MD believed that continued growth was important both for the business and staff motivation. The sales director wished, however, to create for himself a certain 'lifestyle' living.

Gradually, after years of historic agreement, the two founders grew apart and could not agree on future direction. Staff were becoming increasingly frustrated at the lack of new sales and therefore design opportunities.

Unfortunately, the two owners continued to disagree, so much so that folding the company was even considered an option. After eighteen months of argument and negotiation the sales director sold his shares to the MD and left the company.

As a result the company has now extended into new markets and has increased sales to over £7.5 million. Staff are motivated and are enjoying the variety of work and opportunities of both the individual and company growth.

A company is made up of individuals and, while striving for a corporate goal, they still have individual aspirations. These should be respected and encouraged and they will ensure the company's success or failure.

Similarly, if one individual does not appreciate or understand the objectives of the company this could bring the whole company down. Even if they are at senior management level they must be brought in line or let go, irrespective of how difficult this may be to achieve. In this instance, the security and success of the company was felt to be worth fighting for, no matter how difficult it was. (The MD decided his goals and was prepared to pay the price, probably in advance.)

Habit Three: prioritise – do first things first

If you have decided what your end point is, then there is suddenly a clarity about what is and what is not important. Doing the most important things, managing priorities, is management. It is when you are dealing with what is most important that you are using your time most effectively.

Combining clarity about goals and the notion of taking control allows you to choose and ensure that you are being the most effective. If Habit Two is about leadership, then Habit Three is about management.

Examples in practice

- As an individual, you have a finite amount of time and must choose to use it in a way that gives maximum results, based on what it is that you are trying to achieve.
- As a manager, you need clarity about your business goals to ensure that you are doing the most appropriate activities.
- As a business you need to set strategic goals and manage your resources to achieve these goals.

Time management is about understanding what is urgent and what is important – and what is the difference.

All too often, you do not spend enough time in the 'design' phase and spend too much time in the build/do phase of a project. The more time spent in preparation, often the less time you need to spend doing the task. Management is about spending more time thinking and less time doing.

The funeral speech

Imagine you are watching one of those old 1960s movies such as *Blow-Up*. The shots are all very grainy and black and white and it is a dark autumnal day.

The camera pans across a line of people walking across what looks like a park or an open space. The lens focuses on the faces of all the people who are walking as if in a procession. As it catches the faces of the walkers, you realise that you recognise some of them.

You see the faces of old friends and members of your family, your children, and work colleagues. But one face is missing. The face that is missing is your own, because what you are watching is your funeral cortège marching towards your grave to bury you! You are there but you are in your coffin. Maybe this is ten years from now; maybe it is twenty years from now; who knows?

After the funeral there are four speeches: one from a member of your family; one from a friend; one from a work colleague; and one from a member of the society, club, religious institution or worthy cause that you are involved in. Let's consider the first three of these speeches.

Maybe the speech that you get from the member of your family goes something like this: 'He always meant to be a good dad but he always put work first – he was always putting work and money before the children. In fact, when he wasn't working he was drinking or sleeping or working away from home and he used to get overtired and grumpy with everyone around him – he always missed the kids' parents' evenings and he never got to see them when they were playing sport for the school – he was never there when he ought to have been. I'm sure he didn't mean it to end up like this but somehow he lost the plot …'

Maybe the speech from the friend goes: 'He always meant to spend time at home but it never happened that way and what with the work pressure he put himself under, he could never relax in any case – we used to play a lot of guitar and chess together and we used to laugh a lot, but somehow other things always seemed to get in the way and when I did see him he was so grumpy and moody. I don't know quite what went wrong.'

Maybe the speech from the work colleague goes: 'He was always short-tempered and snappy – no one disputed that he was great at his job but he always seemed to resent being at work and he was not what you'd call the best team player. Everything was always such a rush – he never slowed down to enjoy the people or the things around him. I don't know why he felt so out of control.'

If those are the sorts of speech that you think you might get when you imagine the funeral-speech scenario, then maybe it's because the sort of behaviour that you have been displaying deserves it.

Maybe you would like a different set of funeral speeches. Maybe you want your family member to say, 'He was always there on the important occasions and put all the time into the children that he wanted to.' Maybe you want your friend to say, 'He was a great person – always had time for the important things in life. He lived life to the full and always found time for his friends.' Maybe you want your work colleague to say, 'He always did a decent job but he was very clear about what he was happy to do and where and how he drew the line – he was a great person to work with and be with . . .'

If the second set of speeches are the ones that you want then it is not impossible to have them. The point is that the sort of speeches that you will get at your funeral will be the result of how you have lived your life. If you continue behaving as you do at the moment then I am sure that you have a fairly good idea of what sort of speeches you might get.

If, on the other hand, you want a different set of speeches then you must change your behaviour to generate the kind of speeches that you would want. And the big point is that the whole thing is up to you! If you want to change those funeral speeches it is entirely up to you to do something about it.

This is all very sobering stuff – some people consider it hippie rubbish, but I do not. One needs to audit where one is now and decide what it is that one wants. The future is not created at the wave of a magic wand – there is no rule book given to you when you are born, and it is up to you to create your future.

The first three habits, as outlined and discussed above, are internally focused. They look at ourselves and our 'internal' workings, whether we are considering ourselves as an individual, as a manager, or as a business. The next two habits describe how you relate, externally, to the outside world.

Habit Four: think win–win (or no deal)

Win–win is the only sustainable option when dealing with other people. In the long run, customers will not indulge me if my approach is to get to a situation where I win, they lose (win–lose). Likewise, I am not so stupid as to go for an option that says I lose, they win (lose–win). And only in exceptional circumstances would one continue to maintain a relationship where both parties lose (lose–lose).

At a recent seminar, a rather aggressive client (who was also a management consultant) claimed that 'this win–win rubbish' was a load of old nonsense and no one really believed in it. To be quite frank, no one in their right frame of mind would persist in a relationship where there were not benefits to both parties concerned (unless they had some psychopathic tendencies). In the long run it does not make sense to tolerate any other kind of relationship than that of win–win.

There is actually one other position you could find yourself in – this can be described as 'win–win or no deal'. In other words, we say that we would like to be in a position where both parties benefit, but if we cannot reach that position then we should part company on good terms – otherwise we would be trying to impose defeat on the other party. And, we do not want to be in a relationship where the other party, or we, feel exploited. So, the answer is to walk away on good terms.

Examples in practice

 As an individual, you would hope to be in a relationship where both parties get what they wanted out of it, without one partner feeling abused or exploited by the other.

- As a manager, in order to gain the trust and support of your team you must constantly create situations where everyone benefits in order to promote long-term relationships and trust.

- As a business, the real way forward is developing long-term relationships, developing solutions that benefit everybody concerned. Such win-win solutions create an atmosphere of openness and frankness in which future relationships can flourish.

Habit Five: communicate – seek first to understand and then be understood

Often we seem preoccupied with our own needs and don't really pay attention to those people we are meant to be listening to. The standard example is of the husband returning home after a business trip away. He falls into the house and he is full of tales of the journey, the people he has met, the meals he has eaten, the places he has visited – he forgets to ask how things have been at home!

Quite simply, many of us are not very good at listening.

Examples in practice

- As an individual, you need to see things through your family's eyes to understand what they want, otherwise you are imposing your views and solutions on to their situations.

- As a manager, you'd be wise to understand your team members' points of view – to stop and take account of their position may make you reflect and find better, and possibly more satisfying, solutions which benefit all concerned.

- As a business, seeking first to understand is the very essence of marketing. If you listen to what your customers are saying then they will tell you what it is that they really want – and then you can explain how you can help them (but only if you genuinely can). All too often, salespeople lose valuable potential sales because they are too intent on satisfying the first explicit need that they hear, and they don't slow down and listen to the whole of the customer's story, which may include the real causes of the problem.

Habit Six: self-renewal

The final habit, although at the end of the hierarchy, is fundamental to the successful working through of the first five.

There is a story about coming across a woodcutter desperately trying to saw down a tree. If you suggest that the woodcutter take a break and sharpen the saw, he replies that he simply doesn't have the time! This is the same very short-term, upside-down thinking we apply when we try to get home on an almost empty tank of petrol without filling up at a service station.

Self-renewal is about looking after yourselves. To make the rest of the habits work, you need to be fit for the job. If you are not 'up for it' then you will not be able to achieve your primary goals.

Self-renewal comprises four 'pots' that you need constantly to top up. If these pots get too low, then you become unfit or irritable, or at least you will not be operating at your best, which will make the whole process a lot more like hard work.

The pots we are talking about are physical, mental, emotional and spiritual.

Examples in practice

- The physical 'pot'. We all know that we need to take regular exercise, say three or four times a week. This makes you mentally and physically more alert as well as giving you better stamina, overall fitness and a sense of wellbeing. Few of us actually heed the health recommendations and so we feel the cost both now and in the future.

- The mental 'pot'. We know that we work best in short 45-minute bursts and yet so many of us try to convince ourselves that we are doing exceptional work if we start at 8 a.m. and finish at 7 p.m. without taking a break. A swift ten-minute break every hour would clear the brain and stimulate our weary mental faculties. So, why do we insist on working ridiculously long hours, which makes us less and less effective, rather than working smarter?

- The emotional 'pot'. If our emotions have been shaken or dulled by lack of, or excessive (!), stimulation then we become dull and lethargic. We need the time and space that we share with our loved ones to nurture them and to have our own emotions nurtured. We all know how destroyed we feel, both physically and mentally, when our emotional life is falling to pieces.

■ The spiritual 'pot'. For me the spiritual pot does not necessarily have a religious connotation, although for many I know that it does. By spiritual, I mean those things we do that make us more contemplative and reflective about our lives. This may be reached via meditation, prayer, a walk in the countryside, listening to a particular piece of music or reading – whatever it is that is a 'special' and relatively private moment for yourself.

A long period of time ignoring any of the pots will damage your overall wellbeing. Again, the word 'balance' springs to mind in terms of understanding how we approach these issues.

Checklist – being effective

☐ Know what it is it that you are trying to do.

☐ How will you know when you have got there?

☐ Set clear goals with clear time frames.

☐ Is it time to adjust the balance between your private and business life?

☐ Make sure that you are really being effective. For instance, is there anything you should be doing less of? Or anything you should be doing more of?

☐ How could you achieve more of the things that you want?

Frequently asked questions

Q. What has this 'New Age' rubbish got to do with business?

A. Most businesspeople focus so much on their business that they cease to be as effective as they could be. An audit of where we are and where we want to go helps to refocus energies. Some basic principles make us reflect on what we are trying to achieve in all aspects of our lives. Our business will benefit from our being more effective as an individual: clarifying our goals and what we want makes decision making much simpler.

Q. It is all well very spouting out all this theory but in reality, there's no way you could do all this – get real!

A. Yes, the tenets, or habits, may look like a 'new lifestyle'. The reality however is that you can apply the theory – by knowing what you want you are able to start planning. As with all strategy, the habits are all about recognising trade-offs and deciding your goals and being prepared to pay the price.

Q. There's not enough time in the day to do what I am doing now so how do you expect me to do all this?

A. There is no harm in applying the audit–plan–act philosophy to your businesses and to your life. After all, failing to plan is planning to fail. The question is whether you have the patience to apply the habits to your own situation.

Q. It's all a bit goody-goody religious for me. I went to Sunday school when I was a kid and it didn't help me then, so why should I look at this now?

A. Some people do find the 'holier-than-thou' sickly sweet approach of the 'success' commentators to be bordering on some kind of evangelical mission.

Q. I am interested in this stuff; I don't think that this is all hippie rubbish. There is something there and we'd all be fools to deny that we shouldn't spend a bit more time thinking about how we do stuff. What should I do next?

A. Good books to look at would include Stephen Covey's *Seven Habits of Highly Effective People*, Andy Gilbert's *Go Mad*, and Rick Dobbins and Barrie O Pettman's *The Ultimate Entrepreneur's Book*.

Summary

Many of us do not step back and reflect on where we are now and where we are going in terms of our private lives and our careers. Spend time making sure that you are working in the right direction in each aspect of your life.

CHAPTER FOURTEEN

The psychology of success

There are certain things that the successful entrepreneurs do that the others do not. It is as if there were a secret way of the successful. The literature on entrepreneurship is agreed that there are certain traits that most successful entrepreneurs adopt, intuitively or deliberately.

'Innovation' and 'entrepreneurship' are the buzzwords of today. Innovation is all about taking ideas and acting upon them. Entrepreneurship is all about spotting opportunities, gathering the resources and capability, and delivering the idea to market. The difference is often one of semantics. So what is it that the highly successful entrepreneurs do?

The entrepreneur

Entrepreneurship comprises three components:

- Spotting opportunities
- Gathering together the resources
- Building the capability to actually deliver

Most definitions of entrepreneur focus on the spotting of opportunities but the reality is that the gathering of resources and putting in place the machinery to deliver are equally as important.

Using the description above and based on our intuition and experience, we know that entrepreneurs exhibit the following attributes:

- Vision – the ability to see into the future, to imagine how things could be

- Passion – the sheer belief and conviction in one's ideas and actions

- Determination – the willingness to persevere, often against the odds, to create something new where there was nothing

- Communication and delegation skills – the ability to muster the skills and efforts of other people to help to create and deliver a dream; to take something from the imagination and turn it into an actual product or service that people will buy

Listing these attributes does not make them happen and often these characteristics wane in the person trying to drive a company forward.

Key frustrations of business owners

When the business isn't working properly the list of complaints is typically along the following lines:

- Money: not enough profit
- Staff: can't find and keep good people
- Sales: not enough sales or not enough customers
- Stress and time management: the business depends too much on the owner, who doesn't have enough time
- Operations: output is inconsistent in every sense

All of these issues are actually controllable by the owner-manager. The current situation is a result of their behaviour. So the issue is about how to recapture the entrepreneurial spirit, how to retake control. This book is about the tools required but we must also discuss the entrepreneur as a person.

The psychology of success

Successful people have the habit of doing things failures don't like to do. They don't like doing them either, but their disliking is put into second place to the strength of their purpose.

Successful people seem to do things in a different way from the unsuccessful. Success breeds success, and certainly attitude is a key part of the secret of success.

Success is goals

Goals imply ambition and drive. Goals are the motivator that make you work that much harder. Goals give you the reason that you go to work. So be clear about what you want – the lifestyle or the car or the house or the social life. Be clear about what you want to achieve and the focus will help you to succeed.

You will achieve little without goals. List your goals for your business, for your career and for your family. What do you want to achieve? And what will you have to do more of and what will you have to do less of to achieve these goals?

Self-limiting beliefs

What hold us back are our self-limiting beliefs. Our ability to dream is limited by our willingness to allow our imagination its freedom. Fear of failure is drummed into many of us from an early age (others are all too willing to mock our early failures) so that we become nervous to mention our deepest ambitions. Fear of success is another limiter on what you are willing to do.

What's holding you back? What are you frightened of doing that is stopping you from achieving your ambitions? Most fear is mental rather than actual. Fear of flying or of public speaking can be overcome with determination and willpower. How badly do you want your goals? If you aren't prepared to make the necessary sacrifices to achieve your goals, then you don't want them badly enough!

Accept responsibility

The successful accept responsibility for the consequences of their actions. They accept their failures as being a result of their own behaviour and they also accept their successes as being attributable to their own behaviour. They don't blame others.

What business problems are you blaming others for? Accepting responsibility puts you in a position of power – take control of the situation rather than let the situation control you.

Develop a positive attitude

If you surround yourself with negative people you will take on their negativity. In fact, you will absorb the attitudes of those around you. Surround yourself with beer drinkers, and talk about beer and alcohol will soon become the norm. Surround yourself with musicians and talk of music will soon become the norm.

So surround yourself with people and books that stimulate and encourage you to stretch yourself. Do not listen to the doom merchants who transfer their own sense of inadequacy on to you by pointing out all the reasons why you are going to fail.

Believe in yourself

Self-belief and self-confidence are probably the most important gifts we can give to our children. With self-confidence, we are willing to experiment and try out new ideas. We don't measure ourselves by other people's standards.

If you don't believe in what you are doing, then who will? Take yourself seriously. Build up your confidence; challenge yourself and push yourself to do more than just enough. Don't settle for mediocrity: strive to do your best.

Decide to be successful

Success won't just happen to you. You have to work at it. Whatever you want, you can have it but you need to concentrate your efforts to achieve it. You must recognise the trade-offs involved and be prepared to pay those prices.

Decide what your definition of success is. Plan out how you are going to achieve it.

Manage your time

To be successful, you must manage your time as effectively as possible. Many successful entrepreneurs are habitual list makers. You need to manage your time effectively, and to do that you must have clarity about what you are trying to achieve.

Use your time effectively. Do you always use it as well as you could? Cut out the time-wasting activities, decide what is important and concentrate on the activities that give you most benefit.

Set goals and achieve them

Clarity and vision about what you are going to achieve reinforce your determination to succeed. The more you visualise your success, the more you rehearse your victory, so the more you prepare yourself for the task ahead.

What are your goals? What do you want to have achieved in the next three weeks? What do you want to have achieved in the next three months? What is it that you want to have achieved in the next three years?

All successful entrepreneurs have a number of attributes in common, none of which are at all magical. The *Harvard Business Review* once published an excellent study of entrepreneurial qualities by Geoffrey A Timmons. He came up with nine such assets:

1   A high level of drive and energy
2   Enough self-confidence to take carefully calculated, moderate risks
3   A clear idea of money as a way of keeping score and as a means of generating more money
4   The ability to get other people to work with you and for you productively
5   High but realistic, achievable goals
6   Belief that you can control your own destiny
7   Readiness to learn from your own mistakes and failures
8   A long-term vision of the future of your business
9   Intense competitive urge, with self-imposed standards

Checklist – for success

- [ ] Remember, success is goals.
- [ ] What's holding you back? – your self-limiting beliefs.
- [ ] Fundamental rule: accept responsibility.
- [ ] Develop a positive attitude.
- [ ] Believe in yourself.

☐ Decide to be successful.

☐ Manage your time.

☐ Set goals and achieve them.

Frequently asked questions

Q. Are some people born with a success gene or can you be taught how to do it?

A. People are taught how to be successful – and education that inspires self-confidence and self-belief goes a long way to help. Successful people seem to have no common genes; they aren't all brighter or taller. They come in all sorts of sizes and shapes, although having a background that encourages opportunism does seem to help the budding entrepreneur. You can take the steps required to be successful. The first step is to decide to be successful.

Q. Surely success is all about luck, isn't it?

A. Successful people make their own luck. The more you practise, the luckier you seem to get. But you need to be prepared to take the risk. Some people feel too uncomfortable in the 'risk zone'; others relish the experience.

Summary

There are certain behaviours that the successful adopt. The key issue is to decide what success means to you. Armed with that knowledge you can start to achieve your goals.

CHAPTER FIFTEEN

Innovation – getting out of your box

The future of your business depends not on doing the same as everyone else but on being different. In the future it will be the innovative businesses that succeed while the laggards will eventually disappear. The problem may not be how to get innovative thoughts into your mind, but how to get the old thoughts out of your mind, because it is the old ways of thinking that are stopping you from moving forward.

The underlying theme of this book is that you must be different from your competitors. Or else why should customers bother to buy from you at all? If this is the case, then you must spend time creating and emphasising that difference.

Innovation is about doing things differently. You can be innovative in the products you make or you can be innovative in your processes (how you get the products to market).

For example, Blue Vinyl Inc. is unique in its focus on vinyl records from the 1940s and 1950s; it has compiled the largest online catalogue of second-hand and collectors' records. It also has a database of the locations of many of the rarest jazz recordings and access to the stock of a network of second-hand record dealers. These innovative systems make them the first stop for collectors of rare jazz records.

Another example: DollarBrand uses the Internet to bring the latest American surfers' fashions direct from California into the homes of British youngsters, but at UK prices, and with overnight delivery. They no longer need to wait for the main distributors to sell the latest styles.

Stop being incremental

Incrementalism is innovation's worst enemy. All businesses around the world are reaching the limits of incremental change – squeezing another penny out of costs, getting a product to market a few weeks earlier, responding to customers' enquiries a little bit faster, ratcheting quality up one more notch, capturing another point of market share. These are the obsessions of managers today. But pursuing incremental improvements, while rivals reinvent the industry, is like fiddling while Rome burns.

Start looking for large-step change in how you do things. Constant small improvements may no longer be enough. Look at an entire redesign of what you do and how you do it. And look at it through the customers' eyes.

Incremental change creates goals that are slightly stretching. We just try harder to deliver a little bit more. But maybe the original model is at fault. When we seek large, quantum-step improvements then we release our creativity.

Incremental goals do not challenge or stimulate our creativity. If we are asked to reach a book on a shelf at our shoulder height then there is no brainpower or creativity used to reach it. If asked to get a book that is just above our head, then we need to stretch a little to reach it. We just have to try a little harder. If asked to reach a book that is, say, a metre out of our reach, then we come up with all kinds of creative (and maybe crazy) ways to reach the target: use a chair or a ladder, jump up, get on someone's shoulders, abseil from the ceiling, push the bookshelf down.

In business, non-challenging goals create non-creative solutions. Goals need to be challenging to get us thinking creatively.

Left-brain/right-brain thinking

The left hemisphere of the brain predominantly looks after logic, words, parts and specifics – in short, analysis – and is time-bound. It is the preferred thinking style of men. The right hemisphere looks after emotions and rhythm, pictures, wholes and relationships – synthesis – and is time-free. It is the preferred thinking style of women. Maybe this explains some of the difference between male and female managers!

The world we live in is essentially left-brain-dominated: words, measurement and logic have been enthroned; creativity, intuition and artistry have been demoted to second position. It is argued that we live in a world that has been dominated by the masculine. Male-type, left-brain thinking has focused on the numbers. Right-brain thinking, creativity, has taken a back seat.

In any business we need a combination of the two thinking styles. For instance, we need the analytical number crunching to assess the problem. We also need the creativity of the right side of the brain to find original solutions. Ideally, what one would strive for is not the dominance of one over the other, but a balance where the two can complement each other.

To find original solutions, be creative. You can't be a serious innovator unless you are willing to play. Serious fun is not an oxymoron (the juxtaposition of two conflicting ideas such as fighting for peace): it is a necessity. What is interesting is that there is no such thing as an innovative business, only innovative people.

Remove self-limiting beliefs

What's holding us back is our own belief in ourselves. Think dull narrow-minded defeatist thoughts and see what happens. Think crazy thoughts and see what happens. Your job is to play *with* the boundaries rather than *within* the boundaries that we create for ourselves. What is holding us back is ourselves. Choose powerful, not limiting, mindsets.

Real power is not attached to the ownership of knowledge. Real power is in the ability to change mindsets. The ability to change or influence the minds of your colleagues and suppliers and customers is real power. Following on from this, your business must build up its know-how rather than simply its possession of knowledge. Knowledge is useless unless you know how to use it. The recent emphasis on the ownership of knowledge has missed the point that it is what we *do* with the knowledge that really matters.

Keep thinking, 'How can I take this up to a new level? How can I open up the limits?'

The innovation cycle

Getting innovation into your business often poses problems. The innovation cycle is a way to introduce what could be described as institutional innovation. Lasting twelve weeks, an innovation cycle takes a project or idea that can be worked on by a project team alongside their other activities.

Twelve weeks is the right time frame for such an innovation cycle. Any longer and people lose interest in the project; any shorter and the project happens too quickly for there to be any real output or commitment.

Within the twelve weeks of the programme of work, there will be the following stages:

☐ Scan – consider the key issues that you are dealing with. What are the options? For instance, new-product development, a customer survey, improving operational performance, improving staff morale. What are you trying to achieve? How will you determine success? What are your objectives? Where should you be looking for solutions? What resources might you need?

☐ Focus – exactly what are you trying to achieve? What are the key issues that you are trying to deal with? What are the barriers to success? Look at the alternatives. This might be the stage to try out some prototypes or samples to give others a clear idea of what you are trying to do.

☐ Decide – determine what you are going to do. Plan what resources are required and when. Who will be involved and what budget is required?

☐ Act – the implementation stage is where you test out your ideas. In real time you can see if your new and improved technique or product actually works.

☐ Evaluate – the final key stage is to monitor and evaluate performance against what you were hoping to achieve. And then you can review and start all over again if you wish.

Case study

Built to Last, the furniture manufacturers, knew that using expensive craftsmen and traditional processes meant that their factory was slower than their competitors'. As a result, their costs were higher and their profits were simply not enough. An innovation cycle was introduced, looking specifically at the problem. A team comprising the managing director, the sales manager, the factory foreman and a craftsman met for three hours each week to address the problem. The team's journal was as follows:

Scan

Week 1: Identify the problem and definition of a successful project. Identify all competitors and how to find out how they make their goods. Identify key processes in the factory. Identify fastest and slowest craftsmen. Organise customer focus groups to find out what customers value.

Focus

Weeks 2 and 3: Data gathering and brainstorming. Use of a special set of creativity cards to stimulate disconnected thoughts.

Decide

Week 4: Agreement that most processes could be outsourced without affecting quality of the product – costs for making furniture may even reduce if the quality of outsourced jobs is good enough. Craftsmen would spend more time doing the specialist work that they enjoyed most; output of the factory would double.

Week 5: Sample of ten chairs put through system; everyone happy; possibility of a new special 'craftsman' line suggested and a trial ten 'craftsmen' chairs to be made in freed-up time.

Act

Weeks 6 to 10: A hundred chairs per week put through the new system – minor modifications required but new system deemed a success. Second customer focus group confirms this opinion. Unit production cost reduced 25 per cent with no reduction in quality; customer focus group love the special craftsman chairs and talk about a premium price that will exceed standard profit mark-up of 35 per cent.

Evaluate

Weeks 11 and 12: Fine-tuning of the 'standard' and 'craftsman' ranges. Marketing department given the task of putting in place a marketing campaign for the two 'new' lines (this will be delivered in a twelve-week time frame). Team review process: where could they have done better? What would they do differently?

This real example of the innovation cycle in action shows how a simple process can galvanise a team to think up new or better ways to work. Built to Last saw output from the factory increase by 50 per cent per week; profitability returned immediately. Staff were re-motivated as the next innovation cycle team started work on the marketing programme.

The foundations for innovation

1   Make it fun.
2   Listen to your customers and what they want – focus on giving them something extraordinary rather than ordinary.
3   Don't just talk about it: create prototypes so that others can see and touch what you are talking about – strike while the iron is hot.
4   Be clear about whom you are targeting and make sure your innovation will deliver the 'promise', and is easy to understand.
5   Beware the enemy within – the pessimists will always try to defeat your enthusiasm and focus on your fear of failure.

Case study

When Whitby Bird and Company, the structural engineers, were founded in 1984, none of the young partners had been in positions where they had run businesses before.

'I'd never written a cheque outside my own personal expenditure until I had my own business,' says Mark Whitby. 'Everything was on the line. There was a big need to think about how you manage the business.' The answer was to use their engineering skills to run the business.

The partners designed a management system. They persuaded a software writer and his son to help them write a JMS (job-management system), which has grown with the company.

The system takes time sheets and projects and sets out to predict the work you have to do. It then monitors the work done and gives a value for the work against what you are going to get paid.

'It is important,' says Mark, 'because not all jobs achieve the same profit levels. This tells us what we are good at and what we need to change.'

The system has allowed the firm to grow smoothly from three to three hundred in sixteen years. The software is in the hands of teams, not management. The teams can measure their each-month figures compared with the previous-month figures and look for improvements. 'We are,' says Mike, 'able to have as clear an idea as to how well the teams are managing and being managed as the teams do themselves.'

JMS had to be updated for the millennium bug. It was an opportunity to make it completely web-based. This allowed it to be integrated into the firm's regional offices more effectively and for it to be leased to other companies. The software firm that did the updating was so impressed with the product that they started a joint venture with Whitby Bird. The success of a spin-off business, developed through engineering principles but not *about* engineering, has created a culture within the company for other spin-off business ideas to take root. This, in turn, feeds back into the company's well-deserved reputation for innovation.

Checklist – for innovation

- Never underestimate the power of 'helicopter thinking' – look at the issues from above.
- Focus on quantum-step changes rather than incrementalism.
- Visualise the future – use your imagination to create how things could be.
- Communicate your vision, drive and enthusiasm to those you work with.
- Results are the consequence of method and systems plus your determination and intention to succeed.

Checklist – individual characteristics of an effective innovator

To be an effective innovator, you need to:

- Be clear about what you want to achieve
- Define the project aims and benefits
- Be a champion for the project in the eyes of all around you
- Have the courage to take some risks
- Have confidence to make mistakes and learn from them
- Be good at motivating and mobilising others
- Have the persistence to maintain momentum

Checklist – organisational characteristics for effective innovation

The organisational characteristics that encourage innovation are:

- A free flow of information up and down and across the organisation
- A tradition of working in teams and rewarding and sharing credit
- A belief in the value of innovation from the top
- The desire and commitment to put the effort and time required into innovation

Innovation and success

A *Harvard Business Review* article found that the difference between successful and unsuccessful businesses lay in the way that each approached strategy.

The difference was not simply about choosing one analytical tool over another; it was not about choosing one planning model over another. The difference was 'in the companies' fundamental, implicit assumptions about strategy'.

The less successful companies took what can only be described as a conventional approach. Their thinking was dominated by the notion of staying ahead of the competition – matching or beating their rivals.

By contrast, the high-growth companies paid little attention to their rivals. What they *did* do was seek to make their rivals irrelevant! Kim and Mauborgne refer to this as the logic of 'value innovation'.

Conventional strategic logic and the logic of 'value innovation' differ. They differ in the five basic dimensions of strategy. This difference in perception – the type of spectacles through which they view the world, their paradigm – determines which questions are asked, what opportunities are seen and pursued, and how risk is perceived.

The conventional strategic logic

1 Industry and market assumptions: The industry's conditions are seen as given and so strategy is set accordingly.

2 Strategic focus and competitors: Companies often seem to let their competitors set the rules of strategic thinking (a 'follower' mentality is adopted); they compare strengths, weaknesses, opportunities and threats and focus on building competitive advantage.

3 Customers and market segmentation: Growth is often sought through retaining and/or expanding the customer base, which often leads to more and more target segmentation and so specialisation to meet very specific needs.

4 Opportunities and capabilities: Many companies look at what they have got (capabilities) and try to match them to opportunities in the process of working out what they are going to do.

5 Product and service offerings; ourselves: Conventional competition takes place within clearly defined (and traditional) industry boundaries offering clearly defined products and services.

The value-innovation logic

1 Industry and market assumptions: The industry's conditions can be shaped and consequently your strategy will follow your perception (a market-leader mentality is adopted).

2 Strategic focus and competitors: Competition ceases to be the benchmark; because you do not focus on competing, you can distinguish the factors that deliver superior value from all the factors that the industry competes on (order winners rather than order qualifiers). As a result you can make quantum leaps in value offered to dominate the 'market'.

3 Customers and market segmentation: Most customers will focus on real value rather than a slight product differentiation; the value innovator shoots at the core of the market, recognising that some 'niche' customers will be lost.

4 Opportunities and capabilities: Business opportunities are looked at from a clean-slate point of view. You are not constrained by where you are now. As a result you are looking for where the real value-adding opportunity lies and act on that insight.

5 Product and service offerings; ourselves: Rather than being limited by the industry's definition of what you should or should not do, you seek to solve the buyer's major problems across the entire chain even if it takes you into new business. Continually ask where products and services fit into the total chain of the customer's solutions.

Two strategic logics

The five dimensions of strategy	Conventional logic	Value innovation logic
1. **Industry and market assumptions:**	Industry's conditions are given.	Industry's conditions can be shaped.
2. **Competitors and strategic focus:**	A company should build competitive advantages; the aim is to beat the competition.	Competition is not the benchmark; a company should pursue a quantum leap in value to dominate the market.
3. **Customers and market segmentation:**	A company should retain or expand its customer base through further segmentation and customisation; it should focus on the differences in what customers value.	Target the mass of buyers and willingly let some of the existing customers go; focus on the key commonalities in what customers value.
4. **Opportunities and capabilities:**	Exploit existing assets and capabilities.	Do not be constrained by what you already have. Ask, 'What would we do if we started afresh?'
5. **Product and service offerings; ourselves:**	Industry traditional boundaries determine the products and services a company offers; the goal is to maximise the value of those offerings.	Think in terms of the total solution that customers seek, even if that takes you beyond the industry's traditional boundaries.

Case study

Bert Claeys, a Belgian cinema operator, saw video and satellite taking custom away from the cinema, a shrinking market. All cinema operators turned cinemas into multiplexes (ten small screens, plus food and drink). Bert Claeys created Kinepolis: the world's first megaplex, with 25 screens and 7,600 seats. Cinemagoers were offered a radically superior experience without increasing the ticket price (out-of-town sites and little advertising!).

Case study

Accor, the French hotel chain (known for Novotel), imagined a fresh start in the fiercely competitive budget-hotel sectors. They came up with a new concept of a hotel, which led to the launch of Formule 1.

They eliminated standard features such as costly restaurants, 24-hour reception service and lounges, but through high-specification design made rooms soundproof. Rooms are small and equipped only with a bed and the bare necessities.

What you should be asking yourself

1 Which of the factors that your industry assumes as standard could be eliminated? This question forces you to consider whether factors upon which you think you compete actually deliver value to the customer! These factors are normally taken for granted or we get fixated on benchmarking rather than focusing on customer value.

2 Which factors should be reduced well below the industry's standard? This makes you assess whether the product or service has become overengineered as a result of the race to match or beat the competition.

3 Which factors should be raised well above the industry's standard? This pushes you to uncover standards that are not yet satisfying true customer need.

4 Which factors should be created that the industry has never offered? This makes you look for ways to break out of the established ruts in order to discover new ways of adding value to the customer.

Commentary on value innovation

At first sight, the value innovation reasoning appears to argue counter to the perceived knowledge. In fact, it simply confirms what we know already. The orthodox approach to strategy says that you must recognise the high risk attached to new product/market developments (see Ansoff in Chapter Six). This argument remains valid. The value innovators recognise the high risks and high odds but are prepared to take them. As marketers have always preached, they look to the customer base for what the market wants; they adopt a zero-based budgeting approach, starting from first principles. What separates out the examples often used is that they are quantum leaps in the offering delivered to the market.

Strategy is not a one-off happening: it is continuous. Competitors (with similar management education) will naturally arrive at similar strategic solutions; the challenge is to find a different offering that will give you a different strategic approach.

Frequently asked questions

Q. How can you minimise the risks of being innovative?

A. There is always a risk from trying to do things differently. Financial risk is normally matched by the potential gains from profit. If that is not the case then you are doing something wrong.

Q. You talk as if you need to institutionalise innovation – isn't that upside-down thinking?

A. To maintain our sparkle, it is vital that we constantly look to see if there are better ways to do things or better ways to satisfy our customers. If we don't find a better way then someone else will. It seems more sensible to be one step ahead of the game and be the person who is looking for that extra edge. Your customers will reward you and you will gain new customers as a result.

Q. Do customers really want things to be new and ever changing?

A. Some businesses make a virtue of their total lack of innovative behaviour. They actually make a virtue of not being the latest or the fastest. These companies have very cleverly found themselves a unique niche, which many consider vulnerable. Typical businesses include those British ones that extol old family values such as the Morgan Motor Company, Dualit Toasters, Barbour waxed jackets, Quad Electrostatics and Tiptree Jams.

Summary

Being innovative can be frightening. You are asking yourself to go into uncharted territory and there are no guarantees of success. The choice, however, is pretty stark. You cannot afford to sit still and allow the competition to steal a march on you. More and more, wealth is gained from innovation rather than from optimisation; wealth is not gained from perfecting the known but rather from perfecting the unknown.

CHAPTER SIXTEEN

MORFA – Looking at business projects and business plans

This section outlines a framework for looking at business projects and plans. The MORFA framework is currently used by several banking and business support institutions and provides a valuable framework for evaluating new projects. It gets the business to consider and understand what it is trying to do in a project.

Most businesses have plans and ideas that need to be evaluated to ensure that they are valid and that they can stand up to some analysis. The MORFA framework is a tool to assess a business plan or project.

Background

The framework referred to by the acronym MORFA (illustrated in the table opposite) is used to evaluate a project or business proposition, or a business plan. Like the FiMO/RECoIL frameworks, MORFA gives a holistic view of the proposition and enables a more rounded assessment of the project to be made.

The crux of the framework is that, when presented with a business proposition or business idea, you need to consider not only the idea itself but also the person (or people) involved. Both parts of the equation need to be complementary for it to work.

MORFA – for looking at business propositions

When you are trying to assess a start-up or a proposition's potential, it is difficult to determine the feasibility of the project, especially because there are so many unknowns. But, that said, one still needs to try to make a better-informed decision about the credibility of the business plan.

All too often, bankers and investors say, in private, that at the end of the day you 'look 'em in the eye and feel their handshake – that's how you tell whether they're going to make it or not'. This approach seems somewhat unscientific and creates randomness in decision making.

The MORFA framework

When looking at the proposition, we see that are clearly two parts of the equation: the idea and the person, or the people. Under each of these headings is a series of subheadings that essentially make up the MORFA acronym:

The person	The business idea
Objectives	Market
Resources	Objectives
Ability and commitment	Resources
	Financial projections

Component letters of MORFA appear on both sides of the table.

In order to evaluate the concept, you need to see a business plan. The (overused but excellent) definition of a business plan that I like is, 'It enables us to crystallise our thoughts on paper – the process of working out what might happen on paper allows us to make mistakes or discover shortcomings on paper. It is a form of simulation.'

When you look at the business plan and evaluate it, then you use the full MORFA framework to do so. You can consider each aspect of the whole business plan using the subsections (Markets, Objectives, Resources, Financials, Ability).

The business plan
Markets
Objectives
Resources
Financial projections
Ability and commitment of the owner and staff

The MORFA headings in more detail

Markets: What is your product/service? Who will buy it? What is the business environment that you are entering? What market are you entering? What prices will be charged? Who is the competition? How will you sell it?

Objectives: For the person, what are they trying to achieve? What is their motivation? What is their definition of success? For the business, what are the long-term goals and, again, what is the definition of success?

Resources: For the person, what have they done, what do they own and whom do they know that can help them? For the business, what is owned and what can be used to make the business idea come to fruition (physical, human and financial resources)? What are the minimum entry needs into the industry?

Financials: For the person, what are their assets, commitments and liabilities? For the business, how are prices set and what is the cost structure? What do the projected cash-flow and profit and loss forecasts look like? The key issues are economic viability, price and profit.

Ability: For the individual, when looking at ability and skills, look at knowledge, at attitude, circumstances, experience and character.

Using MORFA

In the same way that you marked up the FiMO and RECoIL with scores out of ten for each category, you do the same with MORFA. This gives a broad holistic view and will enable you to see what areas might need more concentration or focus. As you develop the business plan, so you make the prospects more and more reasonable – you reduce the risk as you ensure that your concept has been considered from all angles.

Despite its apparent simplicity as a tool, MORFA never seems to fail to create discussion, debate and better understanding of a proposition's strengths and weaknesses.

MORFA – Assessing the Plan

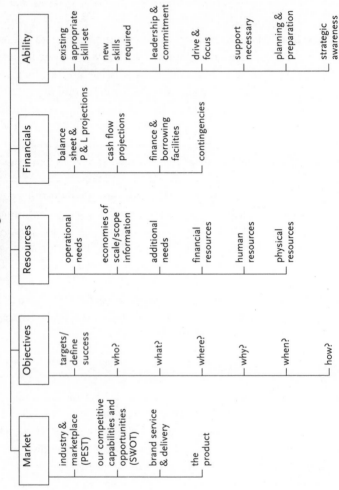

Market
- industry & marketplace (PEST)
- our competitive capabilities and opportunities (SWOT)
- brand service & delivery
- the product

Objectives
- targets/define success
- who?
- what?
- where?
- why?
- when?
- how?

Resources
- operational needs
- economies of scale/scope information
- additional needs
- financial resources
- human resources
- physical resources

Financials
- balance sheet & P & L projections
- cash flow projections
- finance & borrowing facilities
- contingencies

Ability
- existing appropriate skill-set
- new skills required
- leadership & commitment
- drive & focus
- support necessary
- planning & preparation
- strategic awareness

Start-up Framework I

Unknown risk

1 Person

2 Business idea

Objectives
• Motivation
Resources
Ability and skills
• Circumstances
• Experience
• Character

3 Match suitable opportunity

Reasonable prospects

Marketing
• Market
• Environment
• Competition
Resources
• Skills
• Minimum entry needs
Finance
• Economic viability
• Price and profit

Start-up Framework II

Market
• Environment
• Competition
Objectives
Resources required
• Physical
• Human
• Financial
Financial projections
• Controls
• Cash-flow
• Financial structure
Ability and commitment of management

Reasonable prospects

4 Business plan

Measured, acceptable risk

■ A leading high street bank uses MORFA when assessing new businesses and business plans. Bankers see the benefit of using the framework because it is systematic. More importantly, discussing the various key areas adds value to the customer's experience. They realise how the banker can add to their business by asking searching and challenging questions.

■ MORFA was used with an Oxford academic, Peter, who had a brilliant biotechnology business idea. The scientific excellence was not in question. Talking him through MORFA made him come to understand that his brilliant idea fell short on Objectives, and Resources. He had no idea why he wanted to create a start-up. He just thought that it was what he ought to do. Our discussion concluded with his realising that he would be better off staying employed and allowing his academic institution to carry the burden of the 'business side'. He saved himself a lot of heartache.

■ Gerald, an internationally renowned ankle surgeon, was fed up with, in effect, renting clinic and operating space from hospitals. He decided that he wanted to open his own private ankle hospital. The scores were excellent for Markets, Objectives, Resources and Financials. The problem was the Ability and Commitment of Management. As the discussion developed it turned out that he was not prepared to let someone else run his business – and yet he was not prepared to run it himself. The eureka! experience. He realised that what he really wanted to do was spend more time with his patients and not less. In other words, he realised that he did not really want to own and run a hospital. From that moment on, he was able to set about putting together a plan that would enable him to do what he really wanted to do.

Frequently asked questions

Q. Is MORFA for start-ups or for new projects or what?

A. MORFA can be used to look at either start-ups or new business projects. It is a tool for evaluating business plans. There are several business banking institutions who have adapted MORFA to their own needs because it keeps the interview focused on the customer's situation and needs rather than on what the bank wants to find out for its own benefit.

Q. Shouldn't you use MORFA before FiMO/RECoIL?

A. There is no right order for using these tools – you use them how you find them of most benefit. MORFA is best suited for simple start-up or business propositions where there is little track record. Some business thinkers believe that you need to have an idea of what the plan is before you can consider the business capability – they think that MORFA should come before FiMO/RECoIL. I prefer to use FiMO/RECoIL with everything but the newest start-up.

Q. I am not quite sure exactly what score to give for one of the boxes. What should I do?

A. This is a perfectly acceptable state of affairs. The whole purpose of the framework is that it gives you something to discuss. It acts as a tool or as a lever to get you to really start thinking about some of the most basic building blocks of the business. If you can't give a score, it must be because you don't know enough yet and therefore need to do some more talking.

Q. What if I totally screw up on the scoring? It seems that all your examples turned out in failure – it's all doom and gloom!

A. On the contrary. All the framework does is act as a tool for your thinking. MORFA is non-judgemental; it is simply a set of headings for looking at your business plan. Do not blame the messenger. In fact, the more searching and challenging the experience, the better prepared you are for the future.

Summary

MORFA creates a framework for assessing a business proposition. Especially suitable for new business ideas, it acts as a possible alternative to the FiMO/RECoIL framework.

CHAPTER SEVENTEEN

Helping your business to measure up – the scorecard

The Balanced Business Scorecard is an incredibly powerful tool for putting strategy rather than finance alone at the centre of your business. While not appropriate for very small businesses, the process of going through the scorecard gets you to really think through what you are trying to do with your business. It makes you ensure that there is balance between strategic and tactical goals, as well as between the core functions of finance, marketing, operations, and development/learning.

There has been much talk of late about strategy, benchmarking and that we all know that 'what gets measured gets done'. Most businesses are faced by initiative fatigue, and yet there must be some effective route through this quagmire.

The obsessive focus on marketing, teams and strategy is difficult to achieve. Focus on customers and teams is what any winning company tries to do. It is more difficult to focus on strategy.

Strategy is the bridge between what you are trying to do (mission and vision) and doing it (implementation). All too often, companies measure the wrong things (hence the wrong things get done). Alternatively (or, as well!), they have no clear, long-term objectives or goals. As a result, the strategy, the way of getting there, is somewhat confused and ineffective.

If you don't know where you're going, then any road will do

There is a waterfall effect of strategic business planning – a cascade. If you know where you want to be in five years then you will know where you want to be in a year; and if you know where you want to be in a year then you will have a rough idea of what you must do now!

So the goals should be clearly defined, otherwise this planning process cannot take place. A lack of clear goals – or measures that do not reflect goals – will make a nonsense of the process.

This theory is all fine and dandy, but, after you've been on the strategy weekend and written up the business plan, the whole process often starts to fall to pieces. The main reasons for this ineffectiveness are to do with lack of communication and understanding and, more importantly, the lack of relevance of the performance measures to the strategy and mission of the business.

What should you measure?

Performance measures are usually financial; this puts financial control at the centre of the organisation. In effect, you measure what the accountants suggest – and so everyone focuses on those measures. And yet the business comprises marketing and operations functions as well as finance.

Appropriate performance measures can get you into shape. And, the Balanced Business Scorecard (BBS) allows you to measure the right stuff for your business. It is based on the work of Kaplan and Norton.

The Balanced Business Scorecard is a simple technique for putting strategy, not financial controls, at the centre of your business. It makes people in the organisation think about what drives it and shows how results are achieved as well as measuring key indicators for your business and your strategy. So how does it work? If you measure the right stuff then everything should fall into place. (See Part Two, Session Fifteen.)

Balanced business scorecard – the Cascade

To develop the Cascade, you need to follow these steps:

1 Establish the vision – this is the blue-skies idea of how you would like the business to be (in, say, three or five years).

2   Establish the mission – stated in terms such as number of employees, turnover, net profit, number and size of key customers' contracts, key skills and how you wish to be positioned (in say three or five years).

3   Establish your 'competitive' strategy for getting there – after a marketing audit you should be able to select the markets and customers that you wish to sell to; provide a mix of products/services that they value; and do this cheaper or better than your competitors.

4   Establish the milestones (also known as critical success factors, or CSFs) – what do you need to be doing to achieve the strategy (monthly or quarterly)?

5   Establish the performance measures – these measures will reflect your milestones.

The logic behind this 'cascade ' is as follows:

Vision is interpreted as . . . . . .
Mission, which is interpreted in your . . . . . .
Strategy, which is interpreted in your . . . . . .
Milestones (critical success factors), which are interpreted in your . . . . . .
Performance measures.

So, if you hit your performance measures you will achieve your . . . . . .
Milestones, which means that you will achieve your . . . . . .
Strategy, which means that you will achieve your . . . . . .
Mission, which means that you will achieve your . . .
Vision.

So what does the scorecard look like?

At its simplest the scorecard is a sheet of A4 paper with four boxes on it:

1   Finance (or, rather, how the business looks to shareholders)
2   Marketing (or, rather, how the business looks to customers)

3 Operations (or, rather, internal business processes)
4 Innovation/learning perspective (or growth)

Essentially you look for four measures to go in each box, and they can be quantitative or qualitative. They must reflect your milestones.

Balanced Scorecard Explained

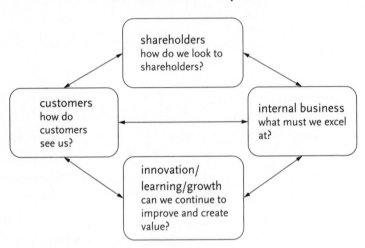

Balanced Scorecard Example: A Small Engineering Works

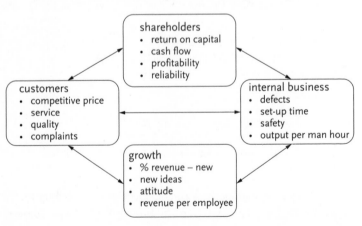

Without going into the detail here, I would like to make a few points about using such a scorecard.

1   This is a dynamic process, constantly updatable.
2   It measures key indicators for your business and your strategy; it measures what is important to you.
3   It is company-wide – the process of establishing the measures means lots of talking and description of vision and mission – translating the vision means clarifying it and gaining consensus.
4   It enables you to set relevant goals and link rewards to those performance measures.
5   It puts strategy (not financial control) at the centre of the business.

The scorecard in practice

To work through the scorecard, you need to work through the action point. This is one of the hardest action points to fill in. While the task looks simple enough to describe, actually doing it is quite tough.

Sample measures: the shareholders' perspective

- ROCE (return on capital employed)[1]
- Gross profit margin
- Net profit margin
- Overheads
- Break-even point
- Cash in hand
- Bank position
- Debtors
- Creditors
- Reliability

---

[1]Although ROCE stands for return on capital employed, you could also use ROSF (return on shareholder funds) or any similar measure of return on your investment in the business.

Sample measures: customers' perspective

- Enquiries
- Proposals accepted/sent
- Contracts started/finished
- Contract size/duration
- New work
- Repeat business
- Customer satisfaction
- Positive image change

Sample measures: internal/operations perspective

- Labour
- Overtime
- Resource utilisation
- Work in progress
- Reject rate
- Maintenance
- Sales per employee
- Complaint rate
- Queues

Sample measures: growth perspective

- Technology leadership
- Manufacturing learning
- Product focus
- Time to market
- Workforce empowerment
- Service innovation
- Partnerships
- Patent applications
- Suggestions from staff
- New products as percentage of output

Case study

Eyes, a retail optician's, used the scorecard to define what it should be trying to do and what it should be measuring. The table below is an abbreviated version of the sort of headings that they decided to use.

Eyes – Strategic Objectives/BBS goals

THE VISION:
'As our customers' preferred provider we shall be the Industry Leader.'

MISSION:
£5m turnover, six outlets, 30 staff, net profit of 10%

THE STRATEGY:
• services surpassing needs
• customers' satisfaction
• employee quality
• shareholder expectations

FINANCIAL GOALS
• ROCE & cash flow
• projected profitability
• performance predictability

SCORECARD GOALS:

CUSTOMER GOALS
• value for money
• competitive price
• innovation

INTERNAL GOALS
• shape customer requirements
• superior management

INNOVATION/LEARNING GOALS
• continuous improvement
• product improvement
• empowered workforce

ACTION POINT

Fill in the gaps below.

Our vision: . . . .

Our mission: . . . .

Our strategy: . . . .

Our milestones: . . . .

Our performance measures: . . . .

Balanced Scorecard

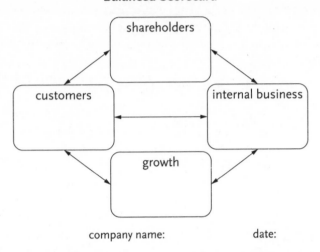

company name: date:

Frequently asked questions

Q. What's the difference between vision and mission?

A. This book is not about getting bogged down in business school definitions! Often I refer to these as Level 1 and Level 2 objectives. Level 1, vision, is essentially the blue-skies picture: what would it feel/look/smell/be like if you were successful; what would you be known for and why and by whom? Level 2, mission, is about the numbers. If you were achieving the vision, then how many employees, what turnover, what net profit, how many clients of what size with what core competency would you have?

Q. I can't fill in the vision box yet, what shall I do?

A. Some find this a really hard exercise. Sometimes it is easier to start with the strategy and then figure out what it is that you are trying to achieve. There are no hard-and-fast rules!

Q. I can't agree with my colleagues what goes into each box. What shall we do?

A. This is common. The process of going through this exercise gets you to discuss and share what you are really trying to do.

If you can start working together then the business gets much easier to run!

Q. Does it matter where you start?

A. It is more logical to start with vision. Strategy is not purely about logic but rather about the process of working through the options and discovering what you do want and what you don't want, so don't worry too much.

Q. How do you transfer from the bottom of the performance measures in the Cascade action point to the scorecard?

A. The list of performance measures will vary from business to business. For the purposes of this exercise, try to carry what you consider to be the key performance measures across to the four-box scorecard so that you end up with no more than four measures in each box. Remember, the whole purpose is to simplify the measuring process so that you are measuring only what really matters. No mean task!

Q. Is this meant to replace regular accounting procedures?

A. No, it should go alongside your regular financial processes.

Q. How often are we meant to do this?

A. It varies. Some businesses, usually with 25+ employees, fall in love with the Cascade and scorecard, and use a monthly scorecard to address how things are going. More commonly, businesses go through the process on an annual basis to remind themselves of what they are trying to do, what they should be measuring, and how it all interrelates.

Q. Does this suit every business?

A. No. It is ideal for any business with more than, say, ten employees, and it comes into its own when businesses employ more than 25 and management feels as if it's starting to lose the plot.

Summary

The Balanced Business Scorecard is a tool for putting strategy, rather than finance, at the centre of your business. It does not suit everyone. The process of going through the scorecard gets you to really think through what you are trying to do with your business.

CHAPTER EIGHTEEN

Crunch questions

Good questions can elicit good, thoughtful and insightful answers. Bad questions tend to generate bad answers. The quest is to be able to select the right questions at the right time. Here is a list of questions that I find incredibly powerful – they precipitate a further analysis of a series of issues and often challenge a series of assumptions, a shaky foundation, upon which a whole empire may have been built.

These questions can be used by the business owner or by an adviser. Several questions can be selected and act as the starting point for an exploratory discussion about the business. Alternatively, you may like to ponder the real answers to these questions. Do not simply give the glib, off-the-cuff answers, but think carefully about what your answers actually imply for the business.

Strategy questions

- What business are you in?
- Where do you make the money?
- How good are your competitive positions?
- Is this a good industry to be in?
- What do your customers think?
- How do you raise profits quickly?
- How do you build long-term value?
- What do you do differently from other businesses?

- What investments underpin your differences?
- What are your key sources of competitive advantage?
- What do you need to do to make a difference?
- What must you keep?
- What must you lose?
- How could you simplify your business so that you could raise value by at least 50 per cent?
- Isn't your strategy rather complex? Aren't all great strategies very simple?
- Does head office/administration destroy more value than it creates?
- What is the key idea, your business concept?

Marketing questions

- Who is your target customer, your client base?
- What do you really know about them?
- Describe a typical customer in detail.
- What problem are you solving?
- Why do people buy your product at all?
- Why do people buy your product from you?
- Why does your typical customer buy from you?
- Which clients are cool?
- Which clients drive you mad?
- Should you be working with them?
- What benefits are you offering that your competition doesn't?
- If you could use just two sentences to describe what your business stands for, what would they be?
- What is your company known for?
- What's your value proposition to customers that they can't get anywhere else?
- Who are your most profitable customers?

- [ ] At what rate do they leave you?
- [ ] Why do they leave?
- [ ] Who is your most serious competitor?
- [ ] What are their plans?
- [ ] What are their costs, profits?
- [ ] Do you really know what customers think about you?
- [ ] Who are currently just new/minor threats?
- [ ] Do you have a product/service that is sharply different from that of your competitors?
- [ ] Are you supplying the right things? And in the most effective way? And at the lowest possible economic cost?
- [ ] Are you as good as or better than your best competitor?
- [ ] Are you serving the widest possible market?
- [ ] Are you in some way unique? Is there a reason why people should buy from you rather than from someone else?

Leadership questions

- [ ] Would God have a good laugh if He saw your business plan?
- [ ] What keeps you awake at night about your business?
- [ ] What are your objectives? What are you trying to achieve?
- [ ] What are the barriers, the obstacles, to achieving your objectives?
- [ ] What will enable you to overcome the barriers, and/or achieve the objectives?
- [ ] If you had a magic wand, what changes would you make to the business?
- [ ] What is stopping you from making your magic-wand changes now?
- [ ] What three things are the most critical to the success of the business?
- [ ] What will you be remembered for?
- [ ] What do you need to do to be memorable?

Financial questions

- [ ] Which 20 per cent of your product makes 80 per cent of your profit?
- [ ] Which 20 per cent of your time makes 80 per cent of the profit?
- [ ] Who are your top five customers and how much contribution did they generate last month?
- [ ] What is the current break-even point?
- [ ] How long can you last if all your current outstanding invoices (debtors) are not paid?
- [ ] How much money are you owed?
- [ ] How much money do you owe?
- [ ] Which customers are unprofitable?
- [ ] Which products should you raise the selling price on now?
- [ ] Which inventory is a waste of space?
- [ ] How can you lower the cost of sales for each product line?
- [ ] Which underperforming product lines should you drop now?
- [ ] Which product lines should you concentrate on selling more of?
- [ ] Which overheads can be reduced sensibly?
- [ ] When did you last check the prices you are paying for your key supplies?

Questions for you

- [ ] Do you ensure that everybody is working together towards agreed and shared objectives?
- [ ] Do you criticise constructively – and praise merit as well as find fault?
- [ ] Do you encourage and organise the generation of new ideas?
- [ ] Do you insist on and organise the highest standards of execution?
- [ ] Do you keep close and productive contact with customers (internal and/or external), suppliers and other parties outside the business?

- [ ] Do you monitor activities continuously, with effective feedback?
- [ ] Do you develop the individual and collective skills of the team and strengthen them as needed by training and recruitment?
- [ ] What is success for you?
- [ ] What is success for the business?
- [ ] What does your business stand for?
- [ ] Is the work you do, exciting or dull?
- [ ] Is what you are doing exciting? Or challenging? Or just plain dull, average and mediocre?
- [ ] So what is it that you do that is so exciting?
- [ ] Does what you do matter?
- [ ] How could you raise the impact?
- [ ] Are you pushing or leading or goading your clients?
- [ ] How do you eat an elephant? Answer: in very small pieces.
- [ ] If your business were an animal, what would it be and why?
- [ ] What animal would you wish your business to be and why?
- [ ] What do you need to do to change your business from the animal that it is to the animal that you wish it were?
- [ ] If your business were an island, what sort of island would it be?
- [ ] Running your business is like riding a bicycle because ...?
- [ ] If you could work half-time, what would you do to double your profit?
- [ ] What would Richard Branson do if he took over your business?
- [ ] What would your closest rival do if they took over your business?
- [ ] What would a raw-meat-eating aggressive capitalist do if they took over your business?
- [ ] What would someone you respect do if they took over your business?
- [ ] Where will you be in three years' time?
- [ ] So, where will you be in one year's time?
- [ ] So what do you need to do now?
- [ ] What excuses do you tend to use?
- [ ] How can you get luckier?

And some crunch one-liners to give you some food for thought

Brand it
You cannot not communicate your brand. Everything about your business communicates something. So what is it that you want to be communicating?

Brand *you*
Treat yourself as a business treats its brand. You need to plan and create a strategy for communicating what it is that you represent, what it is that you do, and where you want to be seen and what you want to be known for. What is your unique selling proposition (USP)?

Sort it – stop procrastinating and do it now
Stop procrastinating. Sometimes it is better to make a decision, one way or the other, and look at the results, rather than make no decision at all. Paralysis by analysis is the disease of the undecided and the uncommitted.

Keep it
Don't make changes for the sake of making changes. If it ain't broke, don't fix it. We spend too much time re-creating, re-engineering things that are perfectly OK.

Get your customers' permission to sell to them
Traditional mass-selling techniques are simply not effective and have low success rates. Look for customers to give you permission to stay in contact with them. Customers who have given you permission to have a relationship with them are ten times more likely to spend money with you.

People love to buy from people, but they hate to be sold *at*
In today's one-to-one marketing world, customers hate to be sold at by badly trained salesmen. But they love to buy products from you. Seduce them to your business but do not treat them like morons.

Establish and control your key indicators

If you don't know where you are going then any road will do! Make sure you are measuring the right stuff. What are you trying to achieve, and will hitting your performance measures enable you to achieve your goals?

Spend a day with weird people

You get out what you put in. If you spend all your time with boring people in boring meetings then you are bound to dampen your creative edge. Somehow your thinking has got to be different from that of your competitors. One of the best ways to sharpen your thinking is to spend some time with people who come at almost everything from a wacky angle. Celebrate the differences and see if you can't find a better way of doing things.

Advise others

The best way to learn is to try to teach others. Work with a business colleague to help to improve his/her business. The process of analysing their business will sharpen the critical skills that you will subsequently apply to your own business.

Lead from the front

Can you lead from anywhere else?

Work the 80/20 principle

The principle of the vital few and the trivial many – 80 per cent of profits come from 20 per cent of customers; 20 per cent of profits come from 80 per cent of customers. If you want to work smarter, focus on the highly effective and ignore the rest!

Strategy is all about trade-offs

Strategy is all about planning while being aware of the business environment. Strategy is about being clear about what you do and what you don't do.

Create marketing space

Separate yourself from the competition. Make yourself different.

Manage the team

Take some responsibility; they won't simply manage themselves.

Remove the wrong people

If you have got the wrong people in post you have three choices. You can sack them, you can train them or you can put up with them. Decide what you're going to do and get on with it.

95 per cent of people earn within 5 per cent of what they think they are worth

People who think they are worth £20,000 a year live, breathe, dress and behave like £20,000-a-year people. They bother to apply only for £20,000-a-year jobs. People who think they are worth £100,000 a year live, breathe, dress and behave like £100,000-a-year people. They bother to apply only for £100,000-a-year jobs. If 95 per cent of people do earn within 5 per cent of what they think they are worth, then how much do you think you should earn?

Remove your self-limiting beliefs

What limits have you set for yourself subconsciously? You are what you believe. If you believe that you cannot swim, then you will not be able to swim. If you believe that you are frightened of flying then you will be frightened of flying. How do you limit yourself?

Stop unprofitable activity

Do you know how profitable you are, by customer, by product, by channel? And if it ain't profitable then why are you doing it? What excuses are you using to continue to do unprofitable work?

Focus on the important

Know the difference between what is urgent and what is important. You must know what things are really important to you or to your business. And, if you know what is really important, then you know what is less important and what is really unimportant. What excuses do you use to work on anything but the most important?

Be first in the customer's mind – and if you can't be first in a category then create a new category

People love to buy from Number One in the category; they believe that Number One is better than the rest (otherwise why would they be Number One?). So you can always be 'Best in the West', 'The first Mexican takeaway', 'The original one-stop shop', 'The only printers with a money-back guarantee' and so forth. If customers love the leader then find a way to lead.

Feel the fear and do it anyway

Fear is a perfectly natural emotion. If you aren't sailing close to the wind then you are probably not taking enough risks. Acknowledge the fear and make a calculated decision. Use the adrenaline and energy that the fear creates to work for you rather than against you.

Infect your staff

Infect your staff with an enthusiasm and excitement for your customers and for the business. Make your staff involved; do not treat them like fools but with the respect that they deserve. After all you can't live out any of your dreams on your own – you need your people to do it for you.

Infect your customers

Delight your customers. Your customers are your most powerful marketing tool. They can get you more business than any multi-million-pound advertising campaign. Get your customers talking about you and being proud to be associated with you and your company.

Seek first to understand, and then to be understood

You have two ears and two eyes but one mouth. When communicating use them in that ratio. Listen, look and speak. You need to understand where your audience is coming from before you can help them. To do any less is highly presumptuous.

Watch your attitude

Your attitude leaks like radioactivity. Everything you do communicates how you feel about what you are doing. So, what messages are you communicating, consciously or unconsciously?

Work on, not in, your business

When Ray Krock started McDonald's, he never intended to work in the business cooking beefburgers: he always intended to work on growing the business. If you work *in* the business then you cannot work *on* the business. How much time do you need to spend working on the business rather than in the business?

Spend more time thinking and less time doing

As you rise up through an organisation you will progressively spend more and more of your time thinking and less and less of your time doing. The role of the leader of an organisation is to spend time looking down on what is going on and taking the broad view.

Less is more – simplify everything

The simpler the concept, the more power it has. Use your time and your resources with care.

Know where you are

Unless you know where you are then how can you map out the route to where you wish to go? Be clear about exactly where you are.

If you don't know where you're going, then any road will do

Unless you know where you are going then how on earth do you expect to arrive there? You will be like a rudderless boat in the middle of the ocean being buffeted by the storms and with no direction home.

Spend more time with outsiders

Customers or suppliers will give you more ideas about your business than five hours in company meetings.

Ask stupid questions

Think the unthinkable and say the unsayable – how else will you be different from your competition?

Stop helping people – let them fail

Only by making their own mistakes will your people learn.

Be better, quicker, cheaper, faster and/or nicer than the competition; focus obsessively on marketing, strategy and teams

Start with the end in mind

Decide your goals, and be prepared to pay the price, probably in advance

You don't get your great ideas sitting at your desk

If you always do what you've always done then you will always get what you've always got

Cut the excuses – just do it

Don't shy away from passion

Keep it simple, stupid!

PART TWO

THE 100-DAY WORKOUT
A strategy workout – your business, your market, your competitors

1 FiMO/RECoIL and SNOW workshop – just how good are you?

2 Vision setting

- Thinking it through in your head
- Thinking it through on a flipchart
- Thinking it through on flipcharts
- Thinking it through your BHAG

3 Key questions in strategy

4 Business purpose audit

5 Market environment audit

6 Competition audit

7 Individual competitor audits

8 Industry attractiveness

9 Culture audit

10 Long-term plans

11 Organisation structure audit

12 Short-term plans

13 Finance workout

14 Bright-marketing workout

- What does your brand say? The one-minute brand test
- What are the benefits to the customers/consumers?
- What business are you in?
- Who is the product for?
- Identify your USP
- What is your position?
- What is your brand positioning statement?
- Guerrilla marketing audit and elevator statement

15 Balanced business scorecard
16 One-page business plan and action planning
17 The best year yet

Outline of the 100-day workout

This 100-day plan can be dipped into or worked through methodically. You can look at each exercise on its own or refer back to the relevant chapters in the text. Good luck!

The 100-day workout is based on work that has been carried out with businesses of all sizes over the last fifteen years. The workout has been applied to both large and small businesses, private and public companies.

How you use the workout is entirely up to you. It is designed to run over roughly fourteen weeks (100 days) so that it does not take up vast quantities of time each week. If you are impatient, the scheme can be condensed and completed within several hours. However, many people find it easier to work on a plan over a longer period of time. You choose how you wish to work with the materials.

Some businesses are happy to work on the materials on their own – some prefer to use an outside facilitator to precipitate and speed things up. You decide. It is your business and it is your future.

The materials have been divided up into sessions. An approximate timing for each session has been indicated along with simple guidelines for running the session – the guidelines are for the benefit of whoever is running it; if you are working on your own, then adjust the instructions accordingly.

Process! Process! Process!

When working through the worksheets, remember why you are doing this.

The purpose of the exercise is not to get through the questions as quickly as possible! You are not at school now.

The purpose of the exercise is to get you to think, discuss, review and develop your ideas and your business. In a world full of quick fixes and Band-Aid solutions, the idea that the best, most appropriate answer may take time (and hard work) has become alien. Do not always accept your first answer. If you want to be brighter, faster, and smarter than the competition then you can't do the same things as they are doing.

Different ways of doing the 100-day workout

Kick-Start gives you all the tools of analysis that you need to transform your business. The hard bit is actually taking your dreams and putting them into action. So, while you are given models and case studies to show you how to kick-start your business, the real part, the serious work, will still have to be done by you. You will need to set aside time to reflect on what you have been doing and what you want to do for the future. More importantly, all the analysis in the world is an entire waste of time without decisions and action. The book, however, will not make it happen. It is you who will do that.

The 100-day workout has seventeen sessions, or exercises, that are estimated to take roughly eighteen to twenty hours if you do them all as instructed. Each session gives an indicative timing and you will adjust this to sort you own needs.

Depending on your specific needs, you can:

> ■ Read Part One first, taking, say, two weeks, and then do the sessions in Part Two at a rate of, say, two a week (for those who are a little more reflective and want to be more thorough).
>
> ■ Go straight to Part Two, the sessions, and plough through them as quickly as possible, and use Part One to check you are approaching the exercises in the right way. This could be done at the speed of, say, three to four sessions per week.
>
> ■ Pick the areas that you think you need to improve and read the relevant section in Part One and do the relevant sessions in Part Two.

Take two full days out of the office and work your way through the sessions as instructed. Spend the remaining 98 days implementing your new plans.

You can choose how to spend the first 100 days. To stick to the 100-day planning concept your time could look as follows:

Week 1:	Scan Part One of the book.
Week 2:	Focus your attention on your key areas for concern in Part One.
Week 3:	Focus and decide – use Part Two sessions to arrive at a plan for the remainder of the period.
Week 4:	Decide and communicate your new plan.
Weeks 5–7:	Act on the plans.
Week 8:	Review progress to date. Celebrate your successes. Learn from your experiences. Adjust plans accordingly.
Weeks 9–10:	Use revised plans to act.
Week 11:	Review progress to date. Celebrate your successes. Learn from your experiences. Adjust or create new plans accordingly.
Weeks 12–13:	Use revised plans to act.
Week 14:	Review progress to date. Celebrate your successes. Learn from your experiences. Adjust or create new plans accordingly.

 Session One

FiMO/RECoIL and SNOW workshop – just how good are you?

Purpose: Agree performance to date and capability to grow. Consider strengths and weaknesses.

Time: Two hours approximately.

Supplies: Flipcharts, copies of the SNOW (standing for strengths, neutrals and weaknesses) and FiMO/RECoIL worksheets for each delegate.

Instructions

1 Talk through the different boxes on the FiMO/RECoIL worksheet (30 minutes). Hand out a worksheet to each delegate.

2 Get each participant to score all the questions on their SNOW worksheet (10 minutes).

3 Get each participant to score all the boxes on their FiMO/RECoIL worksheet (10 minutes) where 0 is a low score and 10 is a high score.

4 In pairs, compare and contrast the FiMO/RECoIL scores that have been put down for the business. Focus on any score of five or less (90 minutes). Ask searching questions of each other; refer to your SNOW scores.

> ■ Why didn't you score higher/lower?
> ■ Where's the evidence to support the score?
> ■ What could be done to improve the scores?

5 As a group compare and contrast your scores (90 minutes).

See page 19 in Chapter One for the FiMO/RECoIL Framework.

SNOW worksheet

SNOW is an excellent set of checklists for clarifying your FiMO and RECoIL scores. SNOW refers to:

> ■ Strengths
> ■ Neutrals
> ■ Weaknesses

Mark the importance of each heading where H is high, M is medium, and L is low.

Mark your strength and the importance of that category to your business. You need good scores for those things that are important to you.

After using the SNOW score sheets you can then decide your FiMO scores. You can also consider the consequences of your SNOW scores.

		strong:	neutral:	weak:	
					importance:
Fi	Turnover	☐	☐	☐	H M L
Fi	Profit	☐	☐	☐	H M L
Fi	Cost structure	☐	☐	☐	H M L
Fi	Balance sheet	☐	☐	☐	H M L
Fi	Cash	☐	☐	☐	H M L
Fi	Ability to raise finance	☐	☐	☐	H M L
Fi	Overhead cost	☐	☐	☐	H M L
M	Products	☐	☐	☐	H M L
M	Pricing	☐	☐	☐	H M L
M	Selling skills	☐	☐	☐	H M L
M	Marketing skills	☐	☐	☐	H M L
M	Quality of brands	☐	☐	☐	H M L
M	Reputation: customers' eyes	☐	☐	☐	H M L
M	Reputation: competitors' eyes	☐	☐	☐	H M L
M	Market share	☐	☐	☐	H M L
O	Quality of staff	☐	☐	☐	H M L
O	Distribution system	☐	☐	☐	H M L
O	Manufacturing skills	☐	☐	☐	H M L
O	Economies of scale	☐	☐	☐	H M L
O	Capacity	☐	☐	☐	H M L
O	Ability to produce on time	☐	☐	☐	H M L
O	Ability to produce to spec.	☐	☐	☐	H M L
O	Ability to customise	☐	☐	☐	H M L
O	Supplier relationships	☐	☐	☐	H M L
O	Customer relationships	☐	☐	☐	H M L
O	Equipment	☐	☐	☐	H M L
O	Technical skills	☐	☐	☐	H M L
O	Human resources management	☐	☐	☐	H M L
R	Access to finance	☐	☐	☐	H M L
R	Quality of HR: management	☐	☐	☐	H M L
R	Quality of HR: workforce	☐	☐	☐	H M L
R	Staff loyalty	☐	☐	☐	H M L
R	Quality of physical assets	☐	☐	☐	H M L
R	Quality of intellectual assets	☐	☐	☐	H M L
E	Appropriate experience	☐	☐	☐	H M L

		strong:	neutral:	weak:	importance:
Co	Approp. controls/systems	☐	☐	☐	H M L
Co	Financial skills: accounting	☐	☐	☐	H M L
Co	Financial skills: management	☐	☐	☐	H M L
Co	IT systems	☐	☐	☐	H M L
Co	Communication	☐	☐	☐	H M L
Co	Organisation structure	☐	☐	☐	H M L
I	Profitable ideas (to market)	☐	☐	☐	H M L
I	Innovative processes	☐	☐	☐	H M L
L	Focus/vision/mission	☐	☐	☐	H M L
L	Business strategy	☐	☐	☐	H M L
L	Ability/commitment: management	☐	☐	☐	H M L

The final part of this process is to establish the following:

> ■ What are the company's top four strengths and what are you going to do with them?
>
> ■ What are the company's top four neutrals and what are you going to do with them?
>
> ■ What are the company's top four weaknesses and what are you going to do with them?

Session Two (Part 1)

Vision setting – thinking it through in your head

Purpose: Develop/agree your vision for the business.
Time: One hour initially.

This exercise is all about dreaming and fantasising about how things could be.

Instructions (to delegates)

Close your eyes and relax.

Recall brushing your teeth this morning. Now, project yourself forward in time. Go forward, a day, a week, a month, a year, two years, three years.

So, now you are looking at yourself in three years' time. It is three years from now and all your plans and dreams have come true. You have been successful.

Imagine opening your eyes and looking at yourself in the mirror as you finish brushing your teeth.

- What are you wearing?
- What does the bathroom look like?
- You walk out of the bathroom to set off to work.
- What does the house look like? Furniture, decorations, lighting, carpets?
- Walk through the house, saying goodbye to any other inhabitants, and go to work by whatever mode of transport you will be using.
- You could be getting into a car: what sort of car?
- What do you look like behind the wheel?
- Look at yourself in the rear-view mirror. You could be walking to a barn in the fields behind your house. You could be getting onto a bike.
- When you arrive at the building where you work, what does it look like? Big? Old? Grubby? Flashy? Postmodern?
- Is there a parking space with your name on it?
- Walk into your workplace. What do you see? Art Deco furnishings or minimalist art? Big vases of flowers? Reception area with a receptionist? Sofas?
- Go to your office space or room where you work. As you walk there, are there rooms full of your staff working on computers or lots of open-plan space?
- A ping-pong room?
- Big fish tanks?
- Cool music being played in the background?
- Big PERT charts on the walls or cartoons?
- And your workroom. What does this look and feel like?

If you can start to imagine the above then you are starting to imagine a scenario of your future vision of work.

Next, write down your vision. Very quickly, jot down in outline what it was like at your workplace of the future (10 minutes).

Now, share your jottings with a colleague. Also, listen to his/her jottings. Compare and contrast your dreams (10 minutes).

Discuss as much of the detail as possible. Make it come alive as you describe it. The more detail that you describe and the more passion and enthusiasm that you put into the exercise, the greater you chance of acting it out.

Session Two (Part 2)

Vision setting – thinking it through on a flipchart

Purpose: Develop/agree a vision for the business.
Time: One hour initially.
Supplies: Flipchart paper and pens, a pile of old Sunday papers, magazines, postcards, glue, Sellotape, crayons, staplers.

This second exercise is an extension of the previous one. After you have done the first 'vision' exercise, you should attempt the following individually.

Instructions

Spend, say, five minutes thinking carefully about what success would be like in about three years. Imagine as much as you can of what it would look, smell and be like if you are successful.

Next, you are going to make a montage of this future success that you have been imagining. If you wish, you can use any images, pictures, headlines from the newspapers and magazines. Or you can draw your future using the flipchart pens. You can spend up to about half an hour assembling 'your future'.

The process of deciding to cut out one picture rather than another helps you use both sides of the brain to decide what you want and do not want in your future. Your choice of images allows you to consider style, quality and values.

Finally, you should share your montage with others. Explain to them why you have chosen the various images and what they represent to you. Allow them to interpret your picture to hear their understanding and perception of what you are trying to do.

Session Two (Part 3)

Vision setting – thinking it through on flipcharts

Purpose: Develop/agree your vision for the business.
Time: One hour initially.
Supplies: Flipchart paper and pens, a pile of old Sunday papers, magazines, postcards, glue, Sellotape, crayons, staplers.

Instructions
Having made your montage of the 'future' you should take another piece of flipchart paper and make a montage of the 'present'.

Finally take another piece of flipchart paper – on a big table lay out the 'present' flipchart, then the blank one and then the 'future' one (from left to right). On the middle flipchart you can now draw/write/
explain how you are going to go from the present to the future.

Session Two (Part 4)

Vision setting – thinking it through your BHAG

Purpose: Develop/agree your Big Hairy Audacious Goal.
Time: One hour initially.

Instructions
In a quiet space fill in the worksheet.

1 What is your core purpose?

2 What are your core values?

3 What is your BHAG?

4 Write out your vivid description.

Session Three

Key questions in strategy

Purpose: Understand and agree the fundamentals of what you are about.
Time: 80 minutes.
Supplies: Flipcharts, copies of the worksheets for each delegate.

Instructions

As individuals and then in small groups consider the following questions. Spend ten minutes on each question.

1 What business are you in?

2 Where do you make the money?

3 How good are your competitive positions?

4 Is this a good industry to be in?

5   What do your customers think about you?

6   What do your competitors think about you?

7   How do you raise profits quickly?

8   How do you build long-term value?

Session Four

Business purpose audit

Purpose: Understand what it is that you are trying to do.
Time: 70 minutes.
Supplies: Flipcharts, copies of the worksheet for each delegate.

Instructions

As individuals and then in small groups, consider the following questions. Spend ten minutes on each question except Question 5, which will deserve at least twice as much time as any of the others – listen carefully to how each person perceives the future!

1   What is the leader's vision of the organisation?

2   The organisation is good at what?

3   How does the organisation treat its employees?

4   How does the organisation treat its customers?

5 What will the organisation look like in three/five years?

6 What core competencies will need to be obtained?

Session Five

Market environment audit

Purpose: Understand and agree what is happening in the market environment.
Time: 40 minutes.
Supplies: Flipcharts, copies of the worksheets for each delegate.

Instructions

As individuals and then in small groups, consider the following questions about how the outside may affect your business, both today and tomorrow. Spend five minutes on each. This audit can be revisited with more accurate information and research. Ask what are:

1 The most important political factors

2 The most important economic factors (domestic)

3 The most important economic factors (abroad)

4 Current demographic trends

5 Current societal/cultural trends

6 Current technological trends

7   The most important legal factors

8   Trends in demand for main services/products

Session Six

Competition audit

Purpose: Understand and agree who are your key competitors.
Time: 30 minutes.
Supplies: Flipcharts, copies of the worksheets for each delegate.

Instructions
As individuals and then in small groups, consider the following questions about your key competitors. Spend five minutes on each question. This audit may need to be revisited with more accurate information and research.

1   Who are the best four performers in the industry and why?

2   Whom do you fear most in each of the top four?

3   Who are the most important regional/other competitors?

4   Who are the customers who could go straight to your suppliers?

5   Who are the suppliers who could go straight to customers?

6   Who might enter your industry?

Session Seven

Individual competitor audits – research work required

Purpose: Gather data about your key competitors.
Time: 1+ hours.

In order to complete the next exercise, the individual competitor audits, you will almost certainly need to do some research to establish the relevant data. At a minimum, some thinking or intelligent guesswork will be required in order to answer some of the questions such that they can add value to your growing understanding of the competitive environment that you are currently working in.

Instructions

Looking at the next session worksheet, gather any information that will help you fill in the sheets for your top four competitors. The questions to be answered for each of your top four competitors concern:

- Revenue and trend:
- Profit and trend:
- Debt/borrowing situation:
- Number of employees:
- Leader's name:
- Preferred method of competing:
- Whether you are satisfied with their current situation:
- How this could be changed:
- What action (of yours) would provoke the fiercest retaliation:
- Key strengths:
- Key weaknesses:

Individual competitor audits

Purpose: Understand and agree what is happening at your top four competitors.
Time: One hour.
Supplies: Flipcharts, copies of the worksheets for each delegate.

Instructions

As individuals and then in small groups, consider the following points. This exercise needs to be done for, say, your key four competitors (15 minutes for each competitor; total, one hour).

Individual competitor audit 1

1   The most important competitor Number One is . . .

2   Revenue and trend:

3   Profit and trend:

4   Debt/borrowing situation:

5   Number of employees:

6   Leader's name:

7   Preferred method of competing:

8   Satisfied?

9   What could change this?

10 What action of yours would provoke the fiercest retaliation?

11 Key strengths:

12 Key weaknesses:

Individual competitor audit 2

1   The most important competitor Number Two is . . .

2   Revenue and trend:

3   Profit and trend:

4   Debt/borrowing situation:

5   Number of employees:

6   Leader's name:

7   Preferred method of competing:

8   Satisfied?

9 What could change this?

10 What action of yours would provoke the fiercest retaliation?

11 Key strengths:

12 Key weaknesses:

Individual competitor audit 3

1 The most important competitor Number Three is . . .

2 Revenue and trend:

3 Profit and trend:

4 Debt/borrowing situation:

5 Number of employees:

6 Leader's name:

7 Preferred method of competing:

8 Satisfied?

9 What could change this?

10 What action of yours would provoke the fiercest retaliation?

11 Key strengths:

12 Key weaknesses:

Individual competitor audit 4

1 The most important competitor Number Four is . . .

2 Revenue and trend:

3 Profit and trend:

4 Debt/borrowing situation:

5 Number of employees:

6 Leader's name:

7 Preferred method of competing:

8   Satisfied?

9   What could change this?

10   What action of yours would provoke the fiercest retaliation?

11   Key strengths:

12   Key weaknesses:

Session Eight

Industry attractiveness

Purpose: An opportunity to reflect on just how attractive your industry is.

Time: 20 minutes.

Supplies: Flipcharts, copies of the worksheets for each delegate.

Instructions

Taking each line, put a tick in one box between the two extremes. For example, if you think that your industry ROCE is around 30 per cent then put a tick in the 'd' column.

When you have answered all eight questions, add up the number of scores in each column. Use the scoring system below to obtain a total score (where each 'a' represents 1 point etc.). The higher the score, the more attractive your industry looks!

Score your industry on the checklist below:

		a	b	c	d	e	
Industry ROCE* (last 5 yrs)	0 per cent p.a.	☐	☐	☐	☐	☐	40 per cent p.a.
Industry ROCE trend	falling	☐	☐	☐	☐	☐	rising
Barriers to entry	very low	☐	☐	☐	☐	☐	very high
Market growth prediction over 5 years	negative	☐	☐	☐	☐	☐	10+ per cent p.a.
Industry capacity	overcapacity	☐	☐	☐	☐	☐	undercapacity
Threat from substitutes	very high	☐	☐	☐	☐	☐	very low
Supplier bargaining power	high	☐	☐	☐	☐	☐	low
Customer bargaining power	high	☐	☐	☐	☐	☐	low
	No. of marks in each column:	a:___ b:___ c:___ d:___ e:___					

Scoring system – a=1; b=2; c=3; d=4; e=5	Total score: . . . . . .
	Possible total: 40

*ROCE stands for Return on Capital Employed.

Session Nine

Culture audit

Purpose: Understand and consider your culture.
Time: 20 minutes.
Supplies: Flipcharts, copies of the worksheets for each delegate.

The culture audit gives you an insight into the type of workplace that you have and so you can consider the 'fit' of your culture with your aspirations.

Instructions
In small groups, spend twenty minutes looking at this worksheet. Keep thinking about the implications of your answers for the business.

1 The three most important events and their effects:
    i)
    ii)
    iii)

2 Main type of work is physical/mental (delete as applicable) labour

3 How do the above affect how you must manage?

4 Most memorable past leader and their behaviour:

5 Most prominent present leader; three words to describe:
   i)
   ii)
   iii)

6 Physical environment of head office:

7 Physical environment of rest of the organisation:

8 You:

are paper-based	☐	or ☐	computer-based
use batch technology	☐	or ☐	process technology
operate on a local scale	☐	or ☐	global scale
are a mature industry	☐	or ☐	new industry
sell a product	☐	or ☐	service

9 Which of the above is the most important and why?

10 Best-known myth in the organisation:

11 Best-known legend:

12 Best-known story:

13 Best-known anecdote:

14 Best-known ritual:

15 Best-known symbol:

16 Best-known travesty:

Session Ten

Long-term plans

Purpose: Write down key plans for the future.
Time: 20+ minutes.
Supplies: Flipcharts, copies of the worksheets for each delegate.

Instructions

Attempt to write your organisation's long-term strategy below, marking out what you will be doing in each year from now. The ease/difficulty that you have writing out these statements will be an indication of how 'sorted' you are. Bearing in mind the earlier worksheets that you have filled in, do the plans make sense? Do they convince you? Because if they do not convince you, then why should they convince anyone else?

What are the organisation's main objectives over the following?

10 years:

5 years:

4 years:

3 years:

2 years:

Organisation structure audit

Purpose: Reflect and consider your organisation structure.
Time: 15+ minutes.
Supplies: Flipcharts, copies of the worksheets for each delegate.

Instructions

Looking at your organisation, fill in the following, deleting as necessary where you see slashes.
Number of employees:
Turnover:
Profits:
Local/regional/national/international
Many/few services/products
Better known for company name/product brands
Centralised/decentralised; lots of rules/few rules
Manager:worker ratio:

Communicate orally/in writing/via email
Consistent service: yes/no
Differing processes: yes/no
Current structure: functional/geographic/product/matrix/mixed
Major advantages:
Major disadvantages:

Session Twelve

Short-term plans

Purpose: Consider the key priorities for the business in the short term.
Time: 15 minutes.
Supplies: Flipcharts, copies of the worksheets for each delegate.

In the coming year, what are your key priorities and how will you measure what it is that you need to achieve in each priority?

Priority 1 (and measures):

Priority 2 (and measures):

Priority 3 (and measures):

If you prefer a less ambiguous approach to this exercise then you can use the four Smart Strategy worksheets below and fill in your priorities on each sheet for the coming year.

1 For financials/shareholders – improving margins and profitability				
Action	Person responsible	Time needed	Due date	How we know it's been done

2 For sales – getting better customers and sales				
Action	Person responsible	Time needed	Due date	How we know it's been done

3 For operations – improving productivity and staff skills				
Action	Person responsible	Time needed	Due date	How we know it's been done

4 For growth – innovation and capability building				
Action	Person responsible	Time needed	Due date	How we know it's been done

Session Thirteen

Finance workout

Purpose: A general look at financials of the business.
Time: 25 minutes.
Supplies: Flipcharts, copies of the worksheets for each delegate.

Instructions

Fill in the following questionnaire to spot any financial alarms that might need to be raised (ticks in the right-hand column suggest some attention may be needed).

1	Are you collecting your debts promptly?	Yes	No
2	Are you straining your creditor relationships?	No	Yes
3	Are you billing promptly?	Yes	No
4	Do you have enough cash?	Yes	No
5	Do you have total control over your costs?	Yes	No
6	Do you have good, long-standing relationships with suppliers?	Yes	No
7	Do you have proper budgets?	Yes	No
8	Are stock levels rising?	No	Yes
9	Are any contracts in dispute?	No	Yes
10	Are you at or near your agreed overdraft limit?	No	Yes
11	Are Final Demands or Writs arriving?	No	Yes
12	Have you communicated your financial plan to all your staff?	Yes	No
13	Do you produce management accounts at least four times a year?	Yes	No
14	Do you compare actual performance with budget?	Yes	No
15	Do you compare actual performance with the previous year?	Yes	No
16	Do you benchmark your performance against industry standards?	Yes	No
17	Do you produce at least a monthly cash statement?	Yes	No

18 Do you monitor key performance indicators:
  – debtor days?   Yes   No
  – creditor days?   Yes   No
  – stock days?   Yes   No
  – gross profit margin?   Yes   No
  – break-even point?   Yes   No
19 Each year, do you seek quotations for:
  – audit?   Yes   No
  – insurance?   Yes   No
  – legal services?   Yes   No
  – banking?   Yes   No
20 Do you invite your bank to discuss your
   business performance, at least annually?   Yes   No
21 Do you acquire information on competitors,
   at least annually?   Yes   No
22 Does your costing procedure tell you the
   margins on each line?   Yes   No
23 Do you use bonus/incentive schemes?   Yes   No
24 Are audited accounts ready within three
   months of year-end?   Yes   No

Dig out your management information systems and work out the following:

1 What is your working capital requirement for the next three years?

2 What is your break-even point, profit centre by profit centre?

3 When did you last increase prices?

4 Which are your most profitable lines?

5   Which are your least profitable lines?

6   What is the net contribution or profit from your top 20 per cent most profitable customers?

7   What is the net contribution or profit from the rest of your customers?

Session Fourteen

Bright-marketing workout

Purpose: Understand and agree what is happening in the business environment and how we fit in it.

Time: 100 minutes.

Supplies: Flipcharts, copies of the worksheets for each delegate.

1 What does your brand say? The one-minute brand test

Take some of your 'branded' materials and give them to ten of your customers and/or potential customers (or imagine how one of your customers would behave!). Get them to spend one minute looking at the materials. In the one minute, the members of the 'focus group' must write down anything that springs to mind about the materials (15 minutes).

> ■ What does it remind you of? (Banks? Skateboarding? Fun? Cricket?)
>
> ■ What does it 'say' to you? (Old-fashioned? Trendy? Retro? Sexy? Dull?)
>
> ■ Who does it appeal to? (Men? Children? Workaholics? Phone users?)
>
> ■ What does it say about the company? (Modern? Grey? Reliable? Design-led?)

2 What are the benefits to the customers/consumers?
Write down the features of your product or service. Next, write
down the benefit (to the customer) of each of the features (10+
minutes).

Features: Associated benefit:

3 What business are you in? (5 minutes)

4 Who is the product for? (5 minutes)

Name specific customers and consumers:

5 Identify your unique selling point (20 minutes)

■ Most suppliers in my industry do the following (a problem):

■ Which means that (a problem for the customer):

■ Well, what we do is (a solution):

■ Which means that (a benefit to the customer) (your USP?):

---

6 What is your position? (20+ minutes)

6a List your competitors and list which customers or customer segments each competitor is aimed at

Competitor: Aimed at:

6b Write down your niche

In other words, which customers or customer segment(s) are you aimed at?

We are aimed at:

6c Establish your position

Establishing your position is a very ambiguous process, which helps you to understand your competitive environment. The position is mapped out in a box/matrix. The box has two different axes that allow you to map out the competing businesses according to how they score according to the axes.

Possible axes:
Style – from formal to informal
Age – from immature to over-mature
Focus – from narrow focus to broad focus

If you plot the two axes on to a matrix and plot the various positions of the differing competitors your map looks as follows:

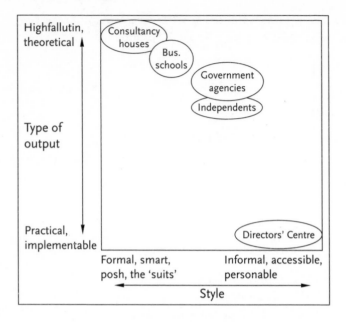

7 What is your brand positioning statement? (25 minutes)

It is worth spending a moment defining the terms in this worksheet. It is the difference in the meanings that enables this worksheet to explore some of the subtlety of what it is that you are trying to get your brand to communicate.

'Market description' is a way of describing the marketplace that the brand is meant to be living in. It is the market description that customers would use. 'Target audience' pinpoints the people you are trying to get to look at your brand, the people you are selling to. 'Brand discriminators' describes the benefits that the brand is best at delivering. 'Core customer proposition' refers to the emotional and functional aspects of what is being offered to the customer. 'Brand differentiators' considers how the brand is different. 'Brand personality' is about the image and associations that it should create.

Brand Positioning Statement (BPS)
Market description:

Target audience:

Brand discriminators:

Core customer proposition:

Brand differentiators:

Brand personality:

8 Guerrilla marketing audit

The final part of the bright-marketing jigsaw is to do a guerrilla marketing audit. Having done the earlier worksheets, you should now have no difficulty in answering these fundamental questions (10 minutes).

1 Who is your target customer?

2 What problem are you solving?

3 What benefits are you offering that your competitors are not?

4 Why should customers spend money with you rather than with your competitors?

5 Two sentences that describe what your business stands for, your elevator statement:

Other associated guerrilla questions
(5 minutes)

- [ ] Will your target audience perceive what you believe to be a competitive advantage as a competitive advantage?
- [ ] Do you offer something different from what your competitors offer?
- [ ] Will people honestly benefit from this advantage?
- [ ] Will they believe your statements about this advantage?
- [ ] Will this advantage motivate people to buy from you?

Session Fifteen

Balanced business scorecard

Purpose: The scorecard puts strategy at the centre of the business.
Time: One hour.
Supplies: Flipcharts, copies of the worksheets for each delegate.

Instructions
To develop the Cascade (see Chapter Seventeen), you need to take the following steps:

1 Establish the vision – this is the blue-skies idea of how you would like the business to be (in say three or five years).
2 Establish the mission – stated in terms such as number of employees, turnover, net profit, number and size of key customers contracts, key skills and how you wish to be positioned (in say three or five years).
3 Establish your 'competitive' strategy for getting there – after a marketing audit you should be able to select the markets and customers that you wish to sell to; provide a mix of products/services that they value; and do this cheaper or better than your competitors.

4 Establish the milestones (also known as Critical Success Factors, CSFs) – what do you need to be doing to achieve the strategy? (Monthly or Quarterly)
5 Establish the performance measures – these measures will reflect your milestones.

Level One: 'Vision': the blue-skies dream of what success would be like, what you would be known as . . .

Which is interpreted in:
Level Two: 'Mission': the numbers – turnover, profits, employees

Which is interpreted in:
Level Three: 'Strategy': how you are going to do it (planning while being aware of the business environment)

Which is interpreted in:
Level Four: 'Milestones': the steps on the way

Which is interpreted in:
Level Five: 'Performance Measures': what you would measure on a weekly/monthly basis

Next, transfer the performance measures from Level Five above to the table below.

Balanced Scorecard

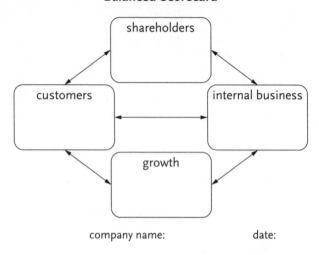

company name: date:

Session Sixteen

One-page business plan and action planning

Purpose: Condense your FiMO/RECoIL, your vision and your key strategies onto one sheet of paper.
Time: One hour.
Supplies: Flipcharts, copies of the worksheets for each delegate.

Instructions

The one-page business plan condenses the whole plan on to one side of paper. Write it up on a piece of flipchart paper for all to see. This is the top-line broad-brush business plan that everyone can see and understand.

The One-Page Business Plan

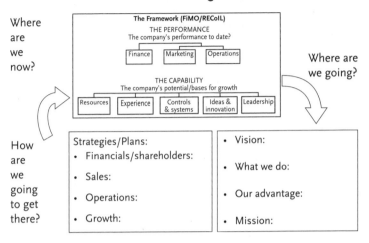

Where are we now?

Where are we going?

How are we going to get there?

Session Seventeen

The best year yet

Purpose: This worksheet addresses your recent personal successes and failures and works on your plans for the future.

Time: One hour.

Supplies: Flipcharts, copies of the worksheets for each delegate.

Instructions

The following worksheet helps you to have your best year yet. Spend some time alone and consider each question, one at a time. By the end you should have a list of actions that you need to carry out.

1 Looking back over your past year, what have been your achievements, and what have you learned from these?

2   Looking back over your past year, what have been your disappointments (your failures), and what have you learned from these?

3   What have been your self-limiting beliefs? What excuses have you made to justify any poor performance? How will you overcome these?

4   List your different roles in life, say, up to eight (e.g., father, husband, MD, coach, boss).

5   For each role, list eight things that you want to achieve in the coming year.

6   Which role is more important than the others?

7   From the lists of goals for the forthcoming year, mark the eight most important ones.

8   For the eight key goals, now address how you are going to achieve them. For each goal:

> - How will you know that you have achieved it?
> - What resources do you need?
> - When will you have completed it?
> - What others things is it dependent on?
> - What are the steps? Work out a timetable.

9   What actions or behaviours have you used to (subconsciously) sabotage your previous efforts to succeed? What things might limit your success and how can you remove them?

Postscript

Although you have now reached the end of the book, you have not reached the end of the journey. You will find that the more that you use these tools, the more benefit they will offer you. You need to use them several times to see the true value of them as tools to illuminate your best way forward.

In order to keep you motivated I suggest the following:

> ☐ Join the Kick-Start discussion forum at
>   www.egroups.com/group/kick-starters
> ☐ Visit the Kick-Starters' website at www.kick-starters.com
> ☐ To see what Robert Craven is currently doing, visit
>   www.robert-craven.com
> ☐ Contact Robert Craven on rc@robert-craven.com

Bibliography

Abraham, J, and Thomson, P, *Fire Your Boss and Hire Yourself*, (Tape), 1997

Armstrong, M, *How To Be an Even More Effective Manager*, 1995

Collins, JC, and Porras, JI, *Built to Last*, 1998

Covey, S, *The Seven Habits of Highly Effective People*, 1999

Craven, R, *Customer is King*, 2002

Davidson, H, *Even More Offensive Marketing*, 1997

Ditzler, J, *My Best Year Yet*, 1996

Dobbins, R, and Pettman, BO, *The Ultimate Entrepreneur's Book*, 1998

Garratt, B, *The Fish Rots from the Head*, 1997

Gerber, ME, *The E-Myth Manager*, 1999

Gilbert, A, *Go Mad*, 1999

Godin, S, *Permission Marketing*, 1999

Hall, D, *In the Company of Heroes*, 1999

Hill, N, *Think and Grow Rich*, 1937

Kaplan, R, and Norton, D, *The Strategy-Focused Organisation*, 2000

Kim, WC, and Mauborgne, R, 'Value Innovation: The Strategic Logic of High Growth', *Harvard Business Review*, January 1997

Koch, R, *Guide to Strategy*, 1995

Koch, R, *The 80/20 Principle*, 1996

Lambert, T, *The Power of Influence*, 1997

LeBoeuf, M, *How To Win Customers and Keep Them for Life*, 1991

Levicki, C, *The Strategy Workout*, 1998

Levinson, JC, & Godin, S, *The Guerrilla Marketing Handbook*, 1995

Maister, DH, *Managing the Professional Service Firm*, 1997

Miles, B, *Paul McCartney: Many Years From Now* , 1997

O'Keefe, J, *Business Beyond the Box*, 1998

Peters, T, *The Circle of Innovation*, 1998

Steiner, R, *My First Break*, 1998

Storey, DJ, *Marketing Success in Fast Growth SMEs*, 1997

Storey, DJ, *The Ten Percenters – Fast Growing SMEs in GB*, 1996

Timmons, GA, *'Business Fundamentals Series'*, *Harvard Business Review*, 15/09/98

Tracy, B, *The Psychology of Achievement – the Phoenix Seminar*, (Tape), 1996

Featured growing companies

Ailsa Hand-made Chocolates
Altruistic
Amanda Barry
Communications
Arcadia
Bert Claeys
Bert Clemens
BJM
Blue Vinyl
Bridget Janes Inc.
Built to Last
Business Systems
Carrick Travel
Directors' Centre, The
DollarBrand
Eyes
Fastbake
Flights of Fancy
Gerry Bentley
Go Mad
Graham and Green
GV2
Happy Computers
Hunter

Improvision
Interaction
Kinneir Dufort
KJ Printing Services
Lighting Company, The
Lumina
Macromedia
Marshall Cummings Marsh
MisterWeb
Motorised Trike Company
MPT Data Collection
Mr Chow's
NJ Filters (NY)
RCA Sound
RHT Outside Catering
Robert's Fudge Factory
Specialist Oils
TKD
Transworld Skate Shop
Tristate Communications
Webbed Design
Whitby Bird & Company
Wild Oats
XTC

Useful websites and addresses

UK government information

Companies House On-Line	www.companieshouse.gov.uk
Competitiveness Unit	www.greatplacetowork.gov.uk
Customs and Excise	www.hmce.gov.uk
Department of Trade and Industry	www.dti.gov.uk
Foresight Knowledge Pool	www.foresight.gov.uk
HM Treasury	www.hm-treasury.gov.uk
Inland Revenue	www.inlandrevenue.gov.uk
Innovation Unit	www.innovation.gov.uk
New Deal	www.newdeal.gov.uk
Office of National Statistics	www.ons.gov.uk
Patent Office and Trade Marks	www.patent.gov.uk

Other UK public bodies

British Chambers of Commerce	www.britishchambers.org.uk
British Franchise Association	www.british-franchise.org.uk
British Standards	www.bsi.org.uk
Building Research Establishment	www.bre.co.uk/brecsu
Connect Business Practice	www.connectbestpractice.com
Design Council	www.design-council.org.uk
Export Trade Directory	www.tradeuk.com
Factors & Discounters Association	www.factors.org.uk
Forum of Private Business	www.fpb.co.uk
LiveWire	www.shell-livewire.org
National Federation of Enterprise Agencies	www.nfea.com
Prince's Trust	www.princes-trust.org.uk
Royal Mail	www.royalmail.co.uk
SOS Export Enquiry Service	www.export.co.uk
Young Enterprise	www.young-enterprise.org.uk

Official UK regulators & ombudsmen

Financial Ombudsman Service	www.obo.org.uk
Financial Services Authority	www.fsa.gov.uk
Insurance Ombudsman Bureau	www.theiob.org.uk
Office of Fair Trading	www.oft.gov.uk
Securities & Futures Authority	www.sfa.org.uk

European information sources

CORDIS EU R&D Programme	www.cordis.lu
EU Information Society Projects	www.ukishelp.co.uk
EUREKA R&D Collaboration	www.eureka.be
Europages Business Directory	www.europages.com
European Commission	www.europa.eu.int
European Info Centres	www.euro-info.org.uk
European Investment Bank	www.eib.org
European Parliament	www.europarl.eu.int
World Chambers of Commerce	www.worldchambers.com

UK professional institutes

Chartered Institute of Marketing	www.cim.co.uk
Institute of Directors	www.iod.co.uk
Institute of Export	www.export.co.uk
Institute of Management Consultancy	www.imc.co.uk
Institute for Small Business Affairs	www.isbauk.org

Business information sources

Audit Bureau of Circulation	www.abc.org.uk
BT Directory Enquiries	www2.bt.com/edq-resnamesearch
Business Zone – SME News	www.businesszone.co.uk
Cobweb Information & News	www.cobwebinfo.com
Entrepreneurial America Inc.	www.entamerica.com
Entrepreneurs Guide (USA)	www.entrepreneurs.about.com
MINTEL Market Research	www.mintel.com
Small Business Admin. (USA)	www.sba.gov
UK Trade Fairs & Exhibitions	www.exhibitions.co.uk
Yellow Pages Directory	www.yell.co.uk

News media

BBC News	www.bbc.co.uk/news
Business 2.0 magazine	www.business2.com

CNN World News	www.cnn.com
Daily Telegraph	www.telegraph.co.uk
Enterprise Network	www.Enterprisenetwork.co.uk
Entrepreneur magazine	www.Entrepreneurmag.com
Fast Company magazine	www.fastcompany.com
Financial Times	www.ft.com
Fortune magazine and *Your Company*	www.fsb.com/fortunesb
News Link – Online Guide	www.newslink.org
News Now – Continuous Feed	www.newsnow.co.uk
News Watch Overview	www.newswatch.co.uk
New York Times	www.nytimes.com
Press Association	www.pa.press.net
Reuters	www.reuters.com/news
Scotsman	www.scotsman.com
Sky News	www.sky.co.uk/news

Company and investment information

Annual Reports Service (*FT*)	www.ibinc.com/ft
City Wire – UK Smaller Shares	www.citywire.co.uk
Companies House On-Line	www.companieshouse.gov.uk
Financial Guide	www.captum.com
Financial Info Net Directory	www.find.co.uk
FreeServe UK Investment Info	www.ukinvest.com
Jordans Online Reports	www.jordans.co.uk
Motley Fool UK – Share Tracker	www.fool.co.uk

Training and development for business advisers

The Directors' Centre	www.thedc.co.uk
Investors in People UK	www.iipuk.co.uk
Learning Direct	www.lifelonglearning.co.uk
Nottingham Business Venture	www.nbv.co.uk
The Shelf repository of T&D information	www.the-shelf.com
Small Firms Enterprise Development Initiative	www.sfedi.org.uk

University business schools

Arkansas Small Business Advice Centre	www.sbaer.uca.edu
Durham University Business School	www.dur.ac.uk/dubs

eCollege Distance Learning	www.ecollege.com
Harvard Business School	www.hbs.edu
Limelight Publishing – case studies	www.limelightpub.co.uk
Strathclyde – business info	www.dis.strath.ac.uk
Ulster – the Management Institute	www.busmgt.ulst.ac.uk
University of St Louis	www.slu.edu/eweb/index
Virtual University for SMEs	www.Vusme.org
Warwick Business School Centre for SMEs	www.wbs.ac.uk/faculty/research/csme.cfm

E-commerce info sources

E-commerce solutions – UK	www.webfusion.co.uk
E-commerce solutions – USA	www.icat.com
E-envoy Government Ambassador	www.e-envoy.gov.uk
InterForum UK Advisory Org.	www.interforum.org
Internet Marketing	www.interbiznet.com/nomad
Internet Marketing & Advertising Association	www.imaa.org
Listing of UK Sites	www.globalcommerce.co.uk
Simpler Trade Procedure Board	www.sitpro.org.uk

Other interesting sites

Business & Skills Direct	www.business-and-skills-direct.co.uk
Business to Business E-commerce	www.mondus.com
Crimson Publishing	www.startups.co.uk

Entrepreneur resources

Discussion Forum for 'Kick-Start Your Business'	www.egroups.com/group/kick-starters
Enterweb	www.enterweb.org
Entreworld	www.entreworld.org
The Innovation Centre	www.theinnovationcentre.com
Kick-Start Your Business	www.kick-starters.com
Robert Craven	www.robert-craven.com
Tom Peters	www.tompeters.com
Virgin Business	www.virginbiz.net

Addresses

Centre for SMEs, Warwick Business School, Coventry CV4 7AL

Chartered Institute of Marketing, Moor Hall, Cookham, Maidenhead, Berks SL6 9QH

Cranfield Business School, Cranfield, Bedford MK43 0AL

The Directors' Centre, 1 The High Street, Woolley, Bath BA1 8AR

Durham University Business School, Mill Hill Lane, Durham, DH1 3LB

etc Limited, Avonmouth House, 6 Avonmouth Street, London SE1 6NX

The Institute of Directors, 116 Pall Mall, London SW1Y 5ED

Glossary of terms

(a set of loose definitions as they have been applied in the book)

Assets: Anything that is owned by the organisation and is leveraged to produce a profit.

Assumptions: Created when we lack facts, and are based on previous experience.

Balance sheet: A snapshot of what the company owns and what it owes.

Balanced Business Scorecard: A simple technique for assessing your goals and evaluating achievement – it puts strategy (not finance) at the centre of the organisation.

Barriers to entry: Obstacles making it difficult or impossible for competitors to enter a particular business segment or market.

Barriers to exit: Undesirable forces that keep too many competitors in a market and lead to overcapacity and low profitability because it is thought to be too expensive to leave.

Benchmarking: Identifying the best performers in the marketplace and comparing your own performance indicators with theirs.

BHAG: Big Hairy Audacious Goal.

Brand: The identity given to a product or corporation through its name and design.

Business Growth Programme: A series of workshops for owner managers usually run by business schools.

Business life cycle: The development of a business over a period of time from growth to maturity and then to decline.

Business plan: A comprehensive written statement setting out where the business is going and how it is going to get there.

Business process re-engineering: Redesigning a company's processes from first principles to improve costs.

Capital employed: The total amount of funds used within the business.

CEO: Chief executive officer.

Competitive advantage: The advantage you have over your rivals – when one player has identified a market or market niche where it is possible to have a price and/or cost advantage over its competitors.

CSF: Core success factor.

Culture: Shared beliefs, attitudes, values and assumptions within an organisation. How you do things.

Culture audit: An analysis of the way the culture affects the organisation.

Differentiation: What makes you different from your competitors.

Director: One who directs and/or leads a business.

Eighty/Twenty Rule (80/20): Pareto's Principle, which states that, in most cases, 20 per cent of inputs generate 80 per cent of outputs – the rule of the vital few and the trivial many.

Entrepreneur: Risk taker who identifies opportunities/gaps in the market, and marshals resource to exploit them.

Entrepreneurship: The process of risk taking.

FD: Finance director.

FiMO: Framework for evaluating business performance to date. It stands for finance, marketing and operations.

Four Ps of marketing: Framework for evaluating marketing strategy: product, place, promotion and price.

Glass ceiling: Point of no further upward movement.

Gross profit (GP): Total amount of profit after direct costs, but before overheads.

Human resource management (HRM): The treatment of your people as a valuable asset.

Innovation: The taking of new ideas (products or processes) and making them happen.

Just in time: Japanese concept, which seeks to reduce stock and have components delivered as and when you need them.

Liquidity: The availability of cash.

Manager: One who manages or supervises other people.

Marginal cost: The additional direct cost of producing one extra unit.

Market segment: A group of (potential/existing) customers that have common characteristics.

Market share: Percentage of buyers of a product or service that choose your company.

Marketing: The concept of identifying and satisfying customers' wants and needs profitably.

MBA: Masters in Business Administration. A university business qualification.

MD: Managing director.

Mission: The numbers that reflect the vision of the business – for example, turnover, number of employees and profit.

Mission statement: A document that details the company's strategic goals in numbers.

MORFA: A framework for evaluating a business proposition or plan: markets, objectives, resources, financials, ability.

NED: Nonexecutive director.

Net profit: The amount of profit after direct costs and overheads have been deducted.

NLP: Neurolinguistic programming – the study of how languages and paralanguage affect thinking and behaviour.

Paradigm: Framework of ideas.

Porter's Five Forces: A structural analysis of the market looking at: the threat of potential new entrants, the threat from substitutes using different technologies, bargaining power of customers, bargaining power of suppliers, and competition among existing suppliers.

Positioning: A market position for a product or a company that separates it from competitors.

RECoIL: A framework for looking at an organisation's capability to grow: it stands for resources, experience, controls and systems, ideas and innovation, and leadership.

ROCE: Return on capital employed – the return on capital spent within an organisation.

SBU: Strategic business unit – a profit centre within a large firm that can be treated as an autonomous unit.

SME: Small to medium-size enterprise typically employing fewer than 250 people.

Strategy: Planning that is done in the light of the business environment.

SWOT analysis: Analysis of a company's strengths, weaknesses, opportunities and threats.

TMS: Target market segment.

USP: Unique selling point or proposition.

Virtuous cycle: A continuously reinforcing cycle of events.

Vision: Where you would like the company to be – a blue-skies statement. An inspiring view of what the business could become.

Vision statement: A clear statement of where the company is going.

Working capital: Cash, accounts receivable and stocks.

Zero-based budgeting: Setting budgets afresh, as if the company were a new start up.

Index

Accor 180
accountants 141
Adair, John 118
advertising 86
Ailsa Handmade Chocolates 98
Altruistic 74
Amanda Barry Communications 32–33
Amazon 35
Ansoff, Igor 81
Ansoff Matrix 81–82, 88
Antoinette, Pierre 106–107
Apple 63
Arcadia 24–25

Balanced Business Scorecard 191–199
  workout 246–248
Barbour jackets 181
Barker, Pete 74
Barry, Amanda 32–33
Beatles, The 113
Ben and Jerry's 35, 83
Bentley, Gerry 40, 79, 83
BHAGs (Big Hairy Audacious Goals) 40–45
BJM agency 145
Blue Vinyl Inc. 169
boards 126–127
Body Shop 35
brand positioning matrix 93–94
brand positioning statement 96–97
branding 77–79, 89–102, 206, 241, 244–245

adding value 98
  Memorable Sensory Experiences 98
Branson, Richard 112
break-even point 136
Bridget Janes Inc. 77
Built to Last 173–174
business environment audit 48–50
business plans 49, 183–189, 248–249
business-unit strategy 62–63, 65, 66
Business Systems UK 56, 137

Caesarea, Jane 24
capital 136
Carrick, Sally 56–59
Carrick Travel 56–59
'Cascade' 192–193
cash flow 131, 135–136, 141
Claeys, Bert 179
Clemens, Bert 40
Coca-Cola 63
communication 159
competitors 52, 76–77, 93, 169, 210
  competition audits 227, 228–231
controls and systems 18, 145–146, 147–148
corporate-centre strategy 62–63, 65, 66–67
Covey, Dr Stephen 151, 152, 162
Crane, Mike 147, 175

Craven's '20:60:20 Rule of Staff
    Development' 103
culture audit 232–234
customer-care plan 108–109
customer charter 107–108
customer initiative programme
    104–105
customer service 105–106
customers 53–54, 78, 206
    brands 90–91
    customer needs 75, 91,
        103–109

decision-making 47–48
delegation 113–114, 119
differentiation of the product 54,
    101
directors 125–129
Directors' Centre 95, 97
Dobbins, Rick 151, 162
DollarBrand 101, 169
Drucker, Peter 47–48
Dualit Toasters 181

Easyjet 35
effectiveness 151–162
elevator statements 99–101
Elmfield, Daniel 114
entrepreneurship 2, 117–118,
    121–123, 163–168
    'serial entrepreneurship' 128
evaluation 9
    performance 10–11, 14
    strategy 55
experience 17
Eyes 197

failure 27–28, 121
Fastbake 25
FiMO 9, 12–16, 55
    workshop 217–220
finance 131–142
    workout 239–241
finance directors 127–128
financial criteria 10–11, 34, 138,
    185

crunch questions 204
'finders, minders and grinders'
    143–144

Garratt, Bob 127
Gibb, Alan 17
Gilbert, Andy 41, 151, 162
glass ceilings 2
global marketing strategy 72
Go MAD 41
goals 40–45, 153–154, 165, 167,
    192, 210
Graham, Antonia 55, 136–137
Graham and Green 55–56,
    136–137
gross profit margin 132–134
growth 2, 16–23, 121–129, 131,
    143–149
guerilla marketing audit 97–98,
    245–246
GV2 146

Haberman, Robert 80–81
Happy Computers 77, 98
Hibbert, Jim 73
Hill, Napoleon 151
Hunter 123–124
Hunter, Lewis 123–124

IBM 41
ideas and innovation 18
Improvision Ltd 98–99
incrementalism 170
industry attractiveness 231–232
innovation 18, 163, 169–182
    foundations 174–175
    innovation cycle 172–174
Interaction 154–155

Jakes, Donald 125
jargon 62, 64
jazz-band leaders 111–117

Kaplan, R. and D. Norton 192
Kennedy, John F. 40
Kim, WC and R. Mauborgne 177

Kinneir, Ross 43–45
Kinneir Dufort 43–45
KJ Printing Systems 41–43
Krock, Ray 209

leadership 18, 26, 30, 111–120
    crunch questions 203
left-brain/right-brain thinking
    170–171
Lennon, John 113
Levi's 98
Lighting Company 100
logos 101–102
Lumina 106–107

Macromedia 77
Maister, David 67, 132, 143
management
    incompetence 28
    jargon 62
management consultants 65
Manchester United 66
market analysis 51, 185
market environment workout
    226–227
marketing 11, 12, 28, 29–30, 32,
    138
    analysing your product 91–92
    Ansoff Matrix 81–82, 88
    branding 77–79, 89–102, 242,
        244–245
    consultants 86–87
    crunch questions 202-203
    global strategy 72
    guerilla marketing audit 97–98,
        245–246
    niches and opportunities
        83–84, 93, 243
    strategy 72–73, 75–79
    target customer groups 53–54
    vision statements 78
    workout 241–246
Marlboro 98
Marsh, Hazel 24
Marshall Cummings Marsh 24
McCartney, Paul 113

McDonald's 209
Memorable Sensory Experiences
    98
Microsoft 63
mission statements 37–46, 143,
    198
MisterWeb 84–85
moon landing 40
MORFA framework 183–189
Morgan Motor Company 181
motivation 30, 108, 119
Motorised Trike Company 14–15
MPT agency 114
Mr Chow's 100

Net Working Capital 136
niches and opportunities 83–84,
    93, 243
NJ Filters 84
non-executive directors 128–129

objectives 67–69, 185
Ohmae, Professor Ken 48
Ono, Yoko 113
operations performance 11, 12
organisation structure audit
    235–236
overheads 135

packaging 77
performance measures 192
PEST analysis of industry 50
Peters, Tom 112
Pettman, Barrie O. 162
planning 47
    workouts 234–235, 236–238
Porter, Professor Michael 48
positive attitude 166
pricing strategy 140
priorities 155
proactive management 152–153
productivity 137–138, 139–140
products and services 75–76, 139
profits 132–135, 138–140
purpose 39
    workout 225–226

Quad Electrostatics 181

RCA Sound 39
RECoIL 9, 16–23, 55
   workshop 217–220
resources 17, 185
responsibility 152–153, 165
RHT 134
Robert's Fudge Factory 80
Roddick, Anita 112

sales and selling price 132–134,
   139
   volume 135
segmentation of the market 54
self-employment 122
self-limiting beliefs 165,
   171–172, 208
self-renewal 160–161
'serial entrepreneurship' 128
SMART goals 62
Smart Strategy Tool 67–69
SNOW workshop 217–220
Sony 41, 63
Specialist Oils 15–16
staff 143–149, 208, 209
   see also teams and people
Starbucks 66, 98
Storey, David 72, 115
strategy 28, 29, 31–32, 47–60,
   138
   Ansoff Matrix 81–82
   approach 61–69
   Balanced Business Scorecard
      191–199
   crunch questions 201–202
   marketing 72–73, 75–79
   pricing 140
   Smart Strategy Tool 67–69
   strategic logic 177–178
   strategic thinking 63–67
   tools and theories 64
   value innovation 177,
      178–179, 180–181
   workout 224–225
success 163–168, 177

surfing 114–118

target customer grouping 53–54,
   66, 93, 101
team leaders 112
teams and people 28, 30–31, 32,
   113, 140
   crisis leadership 117
   customer needs 103–109
   see also staff
Thomson, Peter 151
Thurston, Stephen 56, 137
time management 155,
   166–167
Timmons, Geoffrey A. 167
Tiptree Jams 181
TKD 73
Toshiba 63
Tracy, Brian
Transworld Skate Shop 98

Unique Selling Propositions 101

value innovation 177, 178–179,
   180–181
values 39
Virgin 35
vision statements 37–46,
   198–199
   marketing 78
   workout 220–224

Walmart 41
Walton, Sam 41
Waterfall, Andy 98–99
Watson, Tom Sr 41
Webbed Design 144–145, 146
Whitby, Mark 147, 175
Whitby Bird & Company
   146–147, 175
Wild Oats 124–125
'win-win' 158–159
workplaces 104

XOX formula 124
XTC Ltd 19–23

About the Author

Robert Craven spent five years running training and consultancy programmes for entrepreneurial businesses at Warwick Business School. Running his own consultancy since 1998, he is now one of the UK's best-known and sought-after speakers on entrepreneurship. He is not full of theoretical rhetoric: he offers practical solutions – tangible business results.

Craven's work on marketing and strategy has been widely published and acted upon by thousands of growing businesses – he has been described as 'one of the UK's leading marketing specialists' and 'Mr Entrepreneur'.

Craven's track record in helping businesses is very impressive. Add to this his broad experience at board level and you will understand how and why he uniquely adds value to all the businesses that he works with.

Alongside his numerous speaking engagements, Craven also does consulting work for, and is personal coach to, the leaders of a number of growing businesses in the UK.

Craven runs the Directors' Centre Ltd, which provides consultancy and coaching for growth-minded companies. He can be contacted at rc@robert-craven.com or 00 44 (0)1225 851044. Or go to his website at www.robert-craven.com.

CENTRE FOR SMALL & MEDIUM SIZED ENTERPRISES

Warwick is one of a handful of European business schools that have won a truly global reputation. Its high standards of both teaching and research are regularly confirmed by independent ratings and assessments.

The Centre for Small & Medium Sized Enterprises (CSME) is one of the school's major research centres. We have been working with people starting a business, or already running one, since 1985. The Centre also helps established companies to reignite the entrepreneurial flame that is essential for any modern business.

We don't tell entrepreneurs what to do – just help them be more aware and better informed of the opportunities and pitfalls of running a growing small enterprise.

Much of our practical knowledge is gleaned from the experience of individuals who themselves have been there and done it. These kinds of business coaches rarely commit their observations to paper, but in this Virgin/Warwick series they have captured in print their passion and their knowledge. It's a new kind of business publishing that addresses the constantly evolving challenge of business today.

For more information about Warwick Business School (courses, owner networks and other support to entrepreneurs, managers and new enterprises), please contact:

Centre for Small & Medium Sized Enterprises
Warwick Business School
University of Warwick
Coventry CV4 7AL
UK
Tel: +44 (0) 2476 523741 (CSME); or 524306 (WBS)
Fax: +44(0) 2476 523747 (CSME); or 523719 (WBS)
Email: enquiries@wbs.warwick.ac.uk
And visit CSME's partner website, the Mercia Institute of Enterprise via
www.merciainstitute.com
Tel: +44 (0) 2476 574002

IT'S NOT ABOUT SIZE
BIGGER BRANDS FOR SMALLER BUSINESSES
Paul Dickinson

ISBN 0 7535 0593 2

20/20 HINDSIGHT
FROM STARTING UP TO SUCCESSFUL ENTREPRENEUR, BY THOSE WHO'VE BEEN THERE
Rachelle Thackray

ISBN 0 7535 0547 9

LITTLE e, BIG COMMERCE
HOW TO MAKE A PROFIT ONLINE
Timothy Cumming
ISBN 0 7535 0542 8